D1475186

Te Aotūroa Tātaki

Inclusive early childhood education:
Perspectives on inclusion, social justice
and equity from Aotearoa New Zealand

Edited by

Diane Gordon-Burns, Alexandra C. Gunn, Kerry Purdue
and Nicola Surtees

NZCER PRESS

Wellington 2012

NZCER PRESS

New Zealand Council for Educational Research
PO Box 3237
Wellington

© Diane Gordon-Burns, Alexandra C. Gunn, Kerry Purdue, Nicola Surtees 2012

First published 2012
Reprinted 2012

ISBN 978-1-927151-43-3

Designed by Cluster Creative

Printed by Prestige Print

Coasted Typography Designed by
Willie Devine for House of Aroha

This title is also available as an e-book
from www.nzcer.org.nz/nzcerpress

Distributed by NZCER
PO Box 3237
Wellington
New Zealand
www.nzcer.org.nz

Contents

Forewords

Anne Smith, Emeritus Professor,
University of Otago College of Education

It is an honour to have been invited to write a foreword for this exciting new book on inclusive early childhood education practice. Having been a participant in the history of early childhood education in Aotearoa New Zealand, I am only too aware that we have a great deal to be proud of in our early childhood heritage. Not only are we part of an international trend towards early childhood 'growing up' (Miller, Dalli & Urban, 2012), but we have been leaders in that growing up process. Our pride in this progress, however, comes with some hazards, and this book should play an important role in helping us to avoid stagnation and self satisfaction, and providing impetus for us to become critical and reflective about the ways that we unconsciously exclude some children and families. If it succeeds in doing so, it will build on and enrich our early childhood heritage.

Te Whāriki (Ministry of Education, 1996), the New Zealand early childhood education curriculum, emerged in 1996 from an international trend towards building the economic success of nations on education (May, 2009). In the event, *Te Whāriki* was probably not at all what the policy makers had envisioned, because it is based on holistic principles, empowerment, community knowledge and relationships, rather than any particular drive towards academic success. There is a systematic and serious focus on respecting the Treaty of Waitangi in the document, and the process through which it was developed. Sociocultural theory lies at its heart, acknowledging that children learn collaboratively through the context of their everyday lives and through building on their interests, knowledge and surrounding cultures. Children are constructed as active learners engaged in rich activities and close relationships. Unlike in many other countries, our curriculum is *not* based on a decontextualised positivist construction of children as passive receivers of adult input and socialization strategies, and universalised age and stage-based developmental theories. It emphasises cultural diversity and the importance of all children and families feeling that there is a place for them in early childhood centres:

> Each early childhood education service should ensure that programmes and resources are sensitive and responsive to the different cultures and heritages among the families of the children attending that service. The early childhood curriculum actively contributes towards countering racism and other forms of prejudice. (Ministry of Education, 1996, p.18)

Te Whāriki, therefore, provides a strong foundation to foster inclusive practices which are appropriate for diverse children and families, as advocated within this book. Yet this book shows that we are nowhere near achieving the goal of inclusive practice currently in New Zealand. The success and widespread adoption and endorsement of *Te Whāriki* in Aotearoa New Zealand is unquestionable. But early in its implementation, Joy Cullen (1996) questioned its 'gospel-like status', and the large gap between practice and the ideals of the curriculum. Too many teachers were self-congratulatory about how they were implementing *Te Whāriki*, at the same time as they were using such questionable practices as the use of worksheets, and 'special education' discourses (Cullen, 2004).

To put the principles of *Te Whāriki* into practice it is essential for teachers to have a critical in-depth understanding of theory, and an awareness of the dominant discourses that exist in early childhood centres. Those holding the power and status in early childhood education, at the level of government, and at the level of teacher education, can help to uncover and problematise the accepted truths that underly current early childhood practice. Most important of all, the time and space must exist for teachers to continue to engage in conversations with each other, with children and with participants in their communities, so that hidden ways that exclusion takes place become visible, and so that inclusive strategies to achieve social justice and equity can be fashioned. Diane, Alex, Kerry and Nicola put it into a nutshell when they describe inclusion currently as remaining 'in the realm of rhetoric', and argue that many children and families do not feel accepted and acknowledged in early childhood settings. Their book can help move us from rhetoric to fairness and inclusion.

The content of this book provides excellent material to challenge accepted and unquestioned ideology and discourses that support exclusion. Sonja and Angus Macfarlane argue that Western theories and knowledge have dominated educational research and practice, and point out the challenge of building cultural awareness and incorporating Māori voices into early childhood practice. Richard Manning helps us to understand the necessity for teachers to be culturally competent, and uses a story about the inappropriate use of a haka to illustrate how alienating and disrespectful ignorance can be. Nicola Surtees' chapter argues that the old norm of heteronormativity and nuclear family dominance is totally inappropriate within the context of contemporary diverse constellations of gay and lesbian families. Glynne Mackey and Colleen Lockie raise our awareness of the impact of prevalent economic disadvantage on children, the necessity of giving space and respect to children's views, and helping children and families to ameliorate their poverty. Gina Colvin, Darcey Dachyshyn and Jo Togiaso introduce the disturbing issue of racism and the white colonial discourse that marginalises tamariki and whānau from diverse ethnic backgrounds. Alex Gunn takes the controversial discourse of boys' 'disadvantage' and turns it on its head, by showing the barriers it constructs. Diane Gordon-Burns, Kerry Purdue and colleagues demonstrate that there is still a long way to go before children with disabilities are fully included, despite recent policy changes supporting inclusion. Bradley Hannigan advocates inclusion of religious discourses within early childhood settings.

The book, therefore, has the potential to play a very important role in fostering critical consciousness and awareness of diverse knowledges, values, and lifestyles, and to really make inclusive practice a reality. For children the introduction of inclusive practices in early childhood education will support their diverse identities and give them a great start on understanding their complex world without prejudice or stereotypes. It will give them the opportunity to co-construct wider meanings about fairness, diversity, difference and culture, and will open up more possibilities for their participation and understanding as citizens in a multicultural society. For teachers and teacher educators, the book will enrich their understanding of *Te Whāriki* and stimulate meaningful dialogue about inclusion, as well as help them implement change. This book is an important part of the 'growing up' of early childhood education in Aotearoa New Zealand.

References

Cullen, J. (1996). The challenge of Te Whāriki for future developments in early childhood education. *Delta, 48*(1), 113–126.

Cullen, J. (2004). Adults co-constructing professional knowledge. In A. Anning, J. Cullen & M. Fleer (Eds.), *Early childhood education: Society and culture.* London: Sage Publications.

May, H. (2009). *Politics in the playground: The world of early childhood in New Zealand* (2nd ed.). Dunedin: Otago University Press.

Miller, L., Dalli, C. & Urban, M. (2012). *Early childhood grows up: Towards a critical ecology of the profession.* Dordrecht, Heidelberg, London, New York: Springer.

Ministry of Education. (1996). *Te whāriki: He whāriki mātauranga mō ngā mokopuna o Aotearoa: Early childhood curriculum.* Wellington: Learning Media.

Russell Bishop, Professor of Māori Education,
University of Waikato

I am very honoured to be asked to write a foreword for this book. Initially I was somewhat hesitant to do so, as I have not been part of the development of the specific theorising and practice associated with the development of early childhood education in New Zealand. After reading the contents, however, I am fully engaged because I am part of the wider movement that the editors suggest "has relevance to all sectors of our education system if inclusion is a shared aim" (p. 2).

The denial of a place or voice for Māori and other minoritised students and their families has long been the focus of my work and I am impressed with the way that the authors in this volume seek to address this issue within the wider context of inclusion from their respective domains. They commence with the understanding that despite the promise of *Te Whāriki (*Ministry of Education, 1996), the New Zealand early childhood education curriculum, inclusion remains both difficult to enact and remains in many settings, "at the level of rhetoric" (p. 7). The book addresses the situation created in New Zealand where the dominant discourse is maintained by neo-colonial processes so that "injustice is endemic and systemic, functioning to privilege some groups and marginalise others" (p. 77).

Discourses have a powerful influence on how teachers, and those with whom they interact, understand or ascribe meaning to particular experiences and what eventually happens in practice. Particular discourses will provide teachers with a complex network of explanatory images and metaphors, which are then manifest in their positioning, which then will determine, in large part, how they think and act in relation to indigenous and other minoritised students. In effect, some discourses offer solutions, others merely perpetuate the status quo. The dominance of deficit discourses within early childhood settings limits children's participation and agency when the discourse the teacher is drawing from explains indigenous and other minoritised children's achievement problems in their centres as being due to inherent or culturally-based deficiencies of them or of their parents and families. The relationships and interactions that teachers will develop with these children and their families will be negative; they will engage children in low quality pedagogic content and skill programmes and keep families in subordinate positions. Conversely, if the discourse offers positive explanations and solutions, then teachers will more likely be able to act in an agentic manner—that is, seeing themselves as being able to develop quality caring and learning pedagogic relationships and interactions with indigenous and other minoritised children and their families.

The discursive positioning of self (after Davies & Harre, 1990), a major focus of this book, is a more useful analytic tool than that offered by many theoretical positions. These include theories such as the culturalist position, which promotes pedagogic reform and school/centre culture change, but suffers from a limited consideration of the impact of power differentials within the educational setting and society. The second large group of theorists take a structuralist position, which promotes arguments that being poor or poorly resourced as the result of power differentials within the wider society, inevitably leads to exclusion and poor educational achievement. However, these latter theories give only limited consideration to the agency of educational leaders and policy makers by promoting the argument that there appears little that teachers can achieve in the face of overwhelming structural impediments such as 'school mix' and structural poverty. In contrast, a relational model, such as that offered by an analysis of discursive positioning in terms of power relationships, allows teachers at all levels of the system a means of identifying how society-wide power differentials are played out in classrooms/centres on a day-to-day basis and the part teachers, educational leaders and policy makers themselves may play in the perpetuation of power imbalances and educational disparities.

Such theorising, now almost 20 years since the development of *Te Whāriki*, allows the authors of the chapters in this book the opportunity to critically evaluate, in terms of power relationships, what has become orthodox and comfortable. For example, in chapters 2 and 6, Sonja and Angus Macfarlane and Gina Colvin, Darcey Dachyshyn and Jo Togiaso respectively argue that the traditional instructional and managerial strategies for inclusive education have neglected the centrality of culture to the lives of children. They argue for culture to be at the centre of the ongoing development of theorising around the discourse of inclusion. The latter trio question the dominance of Eurocentric pedagogies and argue for approaches that create situations of cognitive, cultural and/or emotional dissonance for teachers by the provision of evidence that is outside of the usual experiences of the teachers, this evidence being used to critically reflect upon one's discursive positioning and the implications of this positioning for children's experiences and outcomes.

Nicola Surtees also argues that a discourse of diversity must move from the potential that 'normalisation' has for exclusion. Richard Manning's concerns about the usefulness of a culturally appropriate curriculum that promotes seemingly appropriate cultural representations and iconography is part of the promotion of cultural responsiveness by teachers that locates the power to determine appropriateness with the education participants rather than those traditionally in positions of power. Furthering the development of this reappraisal of the discourse on inclusion, Glynne Mackey and Colleen Lockie argue for the agency of early childhood teachers in promoting the self-determination of children and families to strengthen their capacity to address matters that affect them. This is not a denial of the impact of poverty, because they rightly identify that "quality early childhood education programmes ... can never be a panacea for disadvantage and disengagement" (p. 90). Rather they promote the realisation that what early childhood teachers do *now* is important, for example when they regard children as beings in their own right, they promote children's agency and position themselves in power-sharing relationships with children who are then more able to participate in social settings so as to *"actively* practise the skills required for being citizens who are involved in democratic processes" (p. 83), thus inviting active participation and inclusion by children and their families. Alex Gunn challenges essentialised notions of maleness as contributing little to a discourse of inclusion. The potential inclusion, in a discourse of inclusion, of the religious cultures and the religious components of children's cultures by Bradley Hannigan is another call made in this book. Finally Diane Gordon-Burns, Kerry Purdue, Benita Rarere-Briggs, Robyn Stark and Karen Turnock challenge the usefulness of current theorising, policies and practices for ensuring the full inclusion of children with disabilities.

The editors then turn to questioning how the potential for a politics of inclusion in early childhood that appears to be fundamental to *Te Whāriki* has been co-opted in many ways for an exclusionary agenda. They identify the ways in which the authors of this book illustrate how children who represent difference and diversity in our society have instead continued to be 'othered' and minoritised because "people's everyday language and practices build barriers to inclusive education" (p. 175). In this way, this book offers powerful ways of both understanding the dynamics of oppression and marginalisation as well as offering solutions at an individual teacher, centre and systemic level.

Reference

Davies, B. & Harré, R. (1990). Positioning: The discursive production of selves. *Journal for the Theory of Social Behavior, 2*(1), 43–63.

Ministry of Education. (1996). *Te whāriki: He whāriki mātauranga mō ngā mokopuna o Aotearoa: Early childhood curriculum*. Wellington: Learning Media.

Acknowledgements

Producing this book after the devastating 2010/11 Canterbury earthquakes has been an extremely challenging task. Each of the authors, affected in myriad ways by major events in September, December, February and June, has worked tirelessly throughout 2011 to meet, as best she or he could, the demands of an academic and personal life in the aftermath. For those in the city, the challenges of working and living in post-earthquake Christchurch have required constant renegotiation of many aspects of personal and professional lives. Adjustments have been costly in terms of energy, resources and time, so remaining focused on the completion of this book is testament to the authors' commitment to one another, to the profession, and to our collective work for inclusive education.

As editors, we would like to offer our sincere thanks and gratitude to colleagues and friends who have contributed to this book. Each of you made and fulfilled a significant commitment to the project in what has been, for some of you, very difficult circumstances. Your chapters, combining with our own, have allowed us to bring together an array of expertise, knowledge and understanding about inclusive education. We feel privileged that you took up our invitation to contribute: without your willingness to share and persevere, this work would not have been possible. Ngā mihi nui e hoa mā!

We are especially grateful to Paula Wagemaker, contract editor for the University of Canterbury College of Education. Paula, your careful wordsmithing, and guidance and encouragement for the write up and communication of sometimes difficult concepts and ideas, have been greatly appreciated. From beginning to end we have found your editorial and publishing knowledge to be invaluable. Tēnei te mihi Paula.

We would also like to acknowledge some of the New Zealand scholars and activists who, over many years, have been positive role models for us in terms of inclusion, early childhood education, research and collective action. We have learned a great deal from, and would like to recognise, Keith Ballard, Margaret Carr, Anne Smith, Helen May, Joy Cullen, Jude MacArthur, Angus Macfarlane, Tilly Reedy, Margaret Whitford, and Clare Wells. Your contributions to our understandings of inclusion, children's and families' rights, and early childhood education more broadly have been significant. We thank you for your leadership, advocacy and commitment.

We applaud the efforts of children, parents, families, teachers, managers, policy makers, teacher educators, teacher education students and others who are also working hard to counter exclusion, discrimination and inequity in our field. In particular, we thank those who have shared their stories and experiences of difference, diversity, inclusion and exclusion with us in this book. Your experiences have helped us to learn more about what can be done, and what needs to be done, if we are to create more welcoming, accepting and inclusive early childhood education services for all.

Finally, to our partners and families, who have encouraged and supported us while we have worked on this project, thank you.

Di, Alex, Kerry and Nicola.

Glossary

Āhua	demeanour, appearance
ako	children and adults as learners and teachers; the reciprocity of teaching and learning
ākonga	student
Aotearoa	"land of the long white cloud"; a Māori name for New Zealand
hapū	sub-tribe; group of extended families; kinship group
hinengaro	thoughts and feelings; psychological aspects; the mind
hononga	relationships
huakina mai	opening the door—a metaphor for people coming together
huia	a native bird of New Zealand, now extinct
iwi	tribe; a group of sub-tribes
kaiako	teacher
kotahitanga	unity; bonding; holistic development
kuia	an older Māori woman
mana	integrity; respect; dignity; status
Māori	the indigenous people of Aotearoa New Zealand

marae	a traditional and spiritual gathering place within iwi/tribes, where ceremonial events are held, issues are debated and Māori language and customs prevail
mātauranga	education; learning; knowledge
mauri	unique essence; untapped potential
mokopuna	grandchild; child
Pākehā	New Zealander of European descent
papakāinga	land/place to which a person connects; original home base
tamaiti	child
tamariki	children
tangata	person
te reo	the language
te reo Māori	the Māori language
Te Tiriti o Waitangi	the Treaty of Waitangi: a bicultural agreement signed in 1840 between the British Crown and many Māori tribal leaders
Te Whare Tapa Whā	"the four walls of the house": a holistic Māori framework based on the analogy of a strong house, which represents four domains of wellness
Te Whāriki	the early childhood curriculum document

Te Wheke	"the octopus": a holistic Māori framework based on the analogy of the octopus, which represents several domains of wellness
tikanga	customs, protocols
tikanga Māori	Māori customs and protocols
tinana	body; physical aspects
whakapapa	genealogy; lineage; ancestry
whakamana	empowerment
whānau	family; a nuclear or extended family
whānau whānui	extended/wider family
whāriki	woven flax mat
whenua	land

CHAPTER 1

Introduction: Thinking differently about early childhood inclusive education in Aotearoa New Zealand

Diane Gordon-Burns, Alexandra C. Gunn, Kerry Purdue and Nicola Surtees

How do early childhood education settings become places where everyone involved in them can say they feel they belong? What kinds of questions about inclusion, social justice and equity might it be pertinent and productive to ask of contemporary Aotearoa New Zealand early childhood teachers and their practice? When, how and why might teachers intervene to address issues of injustice and exclusion that arise in early childhood work? These are the kinds of questions addressed in this book, which grew out of a need for more information on inclusive early childhood education in this country.

This book also grew out of its authors' strong desire to progress change in early childhood education and thereby make a difference in their own and others' professional and personal lives. All passionate in their own ways about inclusive early childhood education, the authors provide a diversity of research and perspectives on inclusionary and exclusionary practice. The book's contributors, individually and collectively, take the position that if we genuinely want to live with and learn from difference, then people's views, feelings, perspectives and accounts of inclusion, discrimination and exclusion must be told. Putting aside for the moment the multiple ways that cultures, policies and practices can influence one's experiences and interpretations of inclusion—and even what we mean by this term—the contributors see inclusion within educational contexts as an ongoing goal, but not an impossible one.

When planning this book, we, its editors, had several aims. We wanted its content to highlight the need for educational policy makers and teachers to think critically about inclusion and exclusion. This would make more visible the cultures, policies and practices that support or hinder inclusion for all. Sympathetic to relevant national and international developments, we resolved to produce a text that not only moved thinking about inclusive education beyond the traditional focus on special education, but also gave "voice" to multiple viewpoints and experiences. We also wanted this book to contribute to ongoing dialogue about how to bring to fruition an education system where everyone is valued and has his or her rights addressed. Although this book privileges early childhood perspectives, we consider that what is written in these pages has relevance to all sectors of our education system if inclusion is a shared aim.

Throughout this book, we and our colleagues (the book's other authors) have elected to use Māori words in contexts that we and they deem appropriate. The words most frequently used are tamariki (children), whānau (families), kaiako (teachers) and ākonga (students). We also generally preface the English name for our country with its Māori name—Aotearoa. Our reason for this usage aligns with Aotearoa New Zealand's efforts to embrace its responsibilities as a bicultural nation. Those of us working in education have an obligation to uphold the rights of Māori as conveyed in the principles of our country's founding document,

Te Tiriti o Waitangi (the Treaty of Waitangi) and government policy (see, in this regard, Ministry of Education, 1996b, 2009a). As a corollary, we consider that our work should encompass the uniqueness of te reo Māori (the Māori language) as an official language of New Zealand. We agree that we have a duty to promote "te reo and tikanga Māori, making them visible and affirming their value" in our society (Ministry of Education, 1996b, p. 42).

In this introductory chapter our main purpose is to explain the view of inclusion taken in this book. We situate inclusion within the broader legal and policy context for teaching and learning in early childhood education settings in Aotearoa New Zealand. We point out the importance of inclusive education and why we need to keep working for inclusion. We explain the value of engaging with sociocultural and poststructural concepts. These can help us understand the means by which individuals and groups may be privileged, marginalised, judged, included and excluded through everyday language and practices. And we reflect on challenging ourselves and others to engage with cultural politics for change.

Our view of inclusion in early childhood education

The terms "difference", "exclusion" and "inclusion" as applied to people have been theorised in various ways over many years (see, for example, Allan, 2008; Thomas & Loxley, 2001). Each perspective on inclusion—be it essentialist, modernist, social-constructionist, materialist, postmodernist or poststructural—has contributed to shifts in thinking, policy and practice. Of these we consider postmodern and poststructural perspectives to be particularly valuable for the prominence they give to the voices and experiences of marginalised groups. In our opinion, the opportunity to hear what these groups have to say and to "see" what they experience makes the progressing of inclusion ever more possible. Such groups include women; people with disabilities; people identifying as non-heterosexual; people from

Māori, Pasifika and other cultures; children and young people; and others with perceived differences (Carr, Smith, Duncan, Jones, Lee, & Marshall, 2009; Gunn, 2008; Hannigan, 2010; Macartney, 2011; Purdue, 2004; Surtees, 2006; Surtees & Gunn, 2010).

For us, then, inclusion is about the rights of all children, families and adults to participate in environments where "diversity is assumed, welcomed and viewed as a rich resource rather than seen as a problem" (Booth, Nes, & Stromstad, 2003, p. 2). This means, with respect to early childhood education, that all who participate should experience a sense of belonging—a feeling that they are respected and valued for who they are and for what they contribute (Miller & Katz, 2002).

From a practical perspective, inclusive education means taking steps to reduce and eliminate barriers to learning and participation (Booth, Ainscow, & Kingston, 2006). These barriers can be physical, social or conceptual in nature, and eliminating or reducing them requires actively and continually working towards dismantling the values, attitudes and practices that sustain them. This process can only be accomplished through collaborative effort—by addressing exclusion together. Changes in the way we think and interact may be required, as might changes in organisational structures. In this book, the authors discuss relevant issues and suggest some possible ways to proceed. By interrogating notions of difference, exclusion and inclusion from the perspectives of age, sexualities, disability, biculturalism, gender, ethnicity, class/socioeconomic status and religion, their work invites us to enter discussions about how we might construct early childhood communities that allow everyone in them to feel they belong (Ministry of Education, 1996b).

The policy context guiding our inclusive education work

Aotearoa New Zealand is a signatory to various international human rights treaties. These include the United Nations Convention on the Rights of the Child (1989), the United Nations Convention on the Rights of Persons with Disabilities (2006), the United Nations Convention on the Rights of Indigenous Peoples (2007), and the UNESCO Salamanca Statement (1994). In line with this country's commitment to these treaties, the government of Aotearoa New Zealand has, over the last three decades, sought to advance inclusive education by introducing legislation and policy that protects children's rights to free, non-discriminatory and high-quality educational experiences. Our Tiriti o Waitangi, the Education Act 1989 and the Human Rights Act 1993, along with statutory regulations for early childhood education—specifically, the Education (Early Childhood Centres) Regulations 1998 and the Education (Early Childhood Services) Regulations 2008—combine with past and present licensing criteria (Ministry of Education, 1990, 1996a, 2008) and curriculum policy (Ministry of Education, 1996b, 2007) to provide a solid framework for establishing and maintaining inclusive education.

Beyond this provision is a raft of strategies and plans that give effect to the legislated precepts and thereby advance the philosophy and practice of inclusion. Examples include:

- *Quality in Action* (Ministry of Education, 1998)
- *New Zealand Disability Strategy: Making a World of Difference—Whakanui Oranga* (Minister for Disability Issues, 2001)
- *Ngā Huarahi Arataki: Pathways to the Future* (Ministry of Education, 2002)
- *Ka Hikitia—Managing for Success: The Māori Education Strategy* (Ministry of Education, 2009a)
- *The Pasifika Education Plan 2008–2012* (Ministry of Education, 2009b)
- *Success for All: Every School, Every Child* (Ministry of Education, 2010).

Yet, despite this wealth of policy and law, research and commentary show considerable variation in how early childhood centres meet their legislated obligations and responsibilities (see, for example, Gunn et al., 2004; Hannigan, 2010; Macartney, 2011; Minister for Disability Issues, 2001; Purdue, 2004; Terreni, Gunn, Kelly, & Surtees, 2010; Walden, 2011). This body of work highlights the struggle that some in early childhood education still experience as they attempt to provide programmes that enable all children "to grow up as competent and confident learners and communicators, healthy in mind, body and spirit, and secure in their sense of belonging and in the knowledge that they make a valued contribution to society" (Ministry of Education, 1996b, p. 9). This book, through its engagement with diverse perspectives on inclusive, equitable and socially just early childhood education, engages at conceptual and practical levels with the problems and possibilities of "learning about" and "doing" inclusion.

The importance of understanding, promoting and implementing principles of inclusive education

The importance to society of having and valuing an inclusive education system is a recurring theme in this book. Suffice to say at this point that Aotearoa New Zealand's education system has, as evidenced in this book, detrimental effects on those who are excluded. Inclusive education is undoubtedly about recognising and upholding people's rights. It is also about promoting particular values and beliefs; namely, those that contribute to wider understanding and acceptance of and respect for difference and diversity (Allan, 2003).

Discrimination in education has been hard to challenge and change in Aotearoa New Zealand, as in other countries. Dominant neo-liberal and exclusionary discourses portray difference as a disadvantage and as having an inferior and devalued status (Ballard, 1999; Moss, 2010). As Slee (2011, p. 173) states, neo-liberal influence in education

> produces a culture that accepts the inevitability and the justifications for injustice and elitism. This is the kind of education that condemns us to

continue to endure the major problems of our time: sectarian division, environmental degradation, widening gaps between the affluent and the poor, racism, xenophobia, disablism, sexism and homophobia.

Even though Aotearoa New Zealand supports, through policy and legislation, socially just, equitable and inclusive early childhood education, inclusion nevertheless remains difficult to enact. Those of us involved in this area of education can therefore expect to engage in the struggle associated with ensuring that the rights of tamariki and their whānau to fully participate in early childhood settings are met. We are not saying at this point that this country is bereft of settings where these rights are honoured; there are many (see, for example, Gunn et al., 2004). However, as this book and other research highlights, inclusion remains at the level of rhetoric—and sometimes not even that—in a good number of early childhood settings, both here and overseas (Booth et al., 2003). Thus, there are still children and families who experience difficulty having their identities accepted and valued, dreams and aspirations met, and rights as citizens acknowledged and upheld—assuming they have been able to access early childhood education in the first place (Gunn et al., 2004).

We maintain that if we are to bring about inclusion in this country, we must focus on building positive change *early* in children's education, and then progress this foundation of positivity into all educational levels. By developing inclusive early childhood environments with and for very young tamariki and their whānau, we should be able to make a difference to all our lives—not only as participants in early childhood settings but also as full members of communities and society. Central to effecting change is ensuring that negative attitudes towards difference and diversity are countered with new understandings and knowledge. These will help create policies and practices that encourage acceptance and respect, equitable educational opportunities and life chances for all (Moss, 2010; Purdue, Gordon-Burns, Gunn, Madden, & Surtees, 2009; Slee, 2011).

Achieving this state of affairs is not an easy task, of course, because it involves addressing some important attitudinal, theoretical, philosophical, policy and pedagogical issues. It also involves addressing issues related to resourcing, systems and structures. However, the goal of having all tamariki grow up knowing that they and their whānau are positively valued and genuinely included in their communities and societies is far too important for us not to accept the challenge (Ministry of Education, 1996b).

Working for inclusion: Sociocultural and poststructural tools

To delve into the complexities of inclusive education evident in this book, the authors (ourselves included) engage with sociocultural thinking and poststructural practice. The position taken is that knowledge and knowledge construction occur as a result of social processes, not as a result of discovering objective, essential and fixed truths about the world (Burr, 1995; Gergen, 1999). This is a social-constructionist view, and it works for us (the editors) in two significant ways. First, it provides, in the more general sense, an explanation of how individuals and communities form and maintain particular truths, norms, values and beliefs. Second, it recognises that people, individually and collectively, construct their social world and the meanings they ascribe to various phenomena within that world. Accordingly, rather than adopting unreservedly the imposition of a world that exists fixed and external to ourselves and one another, social constructionists view people and the meanings they develop as fluid, dynamic and various. This means that conditions favouring attitudes and practices that include or exclude cannot be seen as static. Thus, inclusion, difference and exclusion in early childhood communities and in society can be variously understood (see, for example, Allan, 2008; Slee, 2011). Moreover, across time, the *normal* state of things can readily change.

The publication in 1996 of *Te Whāriki* (Ministry of Education, 1996b), this country's early childhood curriculum, turned Aotearoa

New Zealand towards cultural-historical perspectives on child development and learning—perspectives that have increasingly informed research, policy and practice (see, for example, Bird & Drewery, 2004; Brennan, 2007; Jordan, 2003; Keesing-Styles & Hedges, 2007; Ministry of Education, 2004/09; Nuttall, 2003). *Te Whāriki* not only provided new frames of reference for comprehending learning and teaching, but it also foregrounded the importance—for early childhood education—of listening to, valuing and drawing on divergent views, values and beliefs about the world. Notions of "learning community" and of "communities of practice" (Lave & Wenger, 1991) became relevant as various individuals and organisations began to reconceptualise the early childhood setting as a place of community engagement, where its members—children and adults alike—could be valued as full participants and as contributors whose points of view matter (Edwards & Nuttall, 2009; Fleer et al., 2006; Gunn et al., 2004; Ministry of Education, 2004/09; Robinson & Jones-Diaz, 2005).

We, the editors, consider that sociocultural thinking and poststructural analyses offer a valuable means of gaining understanding about how such communities function at the local level to include and exclude. Of value is an emphasis on *discourse* for comprehending the ways in which self and the world are constructed, and for identifying the practices that these constructions sustain (Gergen, 1999). Discourses are sets of statements, representations and meanings that construct subjects and objects within particular social, historical and cultural contexts (Burr, 1995).

Discourse forms and produces knowledge and meaning about gender, sexuality, religion, age, class/socioeconomic status, disability, ethnicity and other differences. Various discourses exist for any one topic. Each discourse constructs the topic differently, thereby producing different meanings and knowledge about it, and about how it should be responded to. For example, discourses that define difference as abnormal and undesirable can lead to practices in education that exclude. Inclusion, however, is more likely in contexts in which discourses that draw on the notions of social justice and human rights exist. Such discourses construct difference and diversity as positive and valuable.

There is no particular rule for establishing one discourse's dominance over another. Rather the particular social, political, historical and cultural conditions of a time and place lead to a discourse's ascendancy or competition with another. Whether someone engages with one discourse over another is relative to her or his experiences, beliefs, values and attitudes. These change over time. Often, alternatives become recognised and desired only when one is provoked by an injustice and recognises the play of a dominant discourse in relation to that provocation. As editors, we are conscious that our calls for inclusion may be understood as simply the advancement of a particular discourse. In one sense this would be an accurate reading of our work. However, as we and other authors in this book argue, our stances must be viewed relative to the social, historical, political and cultural contexts that surround them. Our arguments and activism are situated within a convergence today of beliefs, policies and possibilities for advancing social justice and equity with families and young children.

Discourses govern not only what can be thought, written or said about a particular topic, "but also who can speak, when, where and with what authority" (Ball, 1990, p. 17). Those holding to a particular discourse, even if they are not conscious that they are doing so, stake their claim and maintain that what they say holds the most truth and authority. The discourses that become the most visible and accepted are those that most strongly influence our views and beliefs on a subject; alternative discourses are left marginalised or rejected. Certain types of discourses therefore become taken for granted and come to dominate how we construct ourselves and reality.

A great deal of our (Di, Alex, Kerry and Nicola) thinking about discourse can be attributed to the work of the French philosopher, Michel Foucault (1926–1984). His interest in the body and its treatment in the modern era has helped us to comprehend how we, as so-called free-thinking and free-acting human individuals, are involved in marginalising, regulating and normalising ourselves and others in and through our everyday thoughts, language and interactions (Allan, 2008).

From a Foucauldian perspective, power, knowledge and the body are inextricably enmeshed. Foucault viewed power as being everywhere and as productive of the conditions through which lives would be lived. Power is present in what Foucault (1977, p. 137) called "disciplines", and is thus seen in disciplinary practices or techniques that attempt to "improve the imperfect person" (Gergen, 1999, p. 206). Techniques of *surveillance, normalising judgements* and *examination*, for instance, function to produce "docile bodies" (Foucault, 1977, p. 138). These are people who, whether singly or in groups, willingly subject themselves to the regulation, domination and control of various other individuals and groups who want to mould them into specific kinds of people (Burr, 1995). The techniques or practices are also used by individuals as they subject themselves to their own self-scrutiny. Allan's (2008) summary of these disciplinary practices is pertinent to the discussions in this book:

Surveillance: the expert and normalising gaze on people that makes it possible for populations to be judged, classified and controlled;

Normalising judgements: standards of 'normality' (the perfect body, the normal child, the healthy mind) that are used to highlight differences or abnormalities amongst individuals and that seek to eradicate those differences through medicalisation, objectification, treatment, confinement and exclusion; and

Examination: written documentation or assessments that ascertain where the individual differs from the norm and what interventions need to occur to make the person more 'normal'. (pp. 86–87)

The establishment of standards by which we judge and are judged occurs discursively because they reflect the dominant values, attitudes and beliefs accepted and in circulation. This occurrence suggests that individuals' experiences of domination and oppression are mediated by the workings of power rather than by a "neatly packaged, one size fits all" imposition of power. The chapters in this book, individually and collectively, illustrate such processes as their authors consider how to achieve socially just, equitable and inclusive early childhood education.

We, the editors, also consider discourse analysis to be a useful tool for identifying the constructions that people use to talk about difference and diversity and that inform their associated responses, actions and practices. Because we are attempting to point out and oppose the continuance of discourses in early childhood education that discriminate, oppress and exclude, our approach is one that is focused on cultural politics. It therefore aligns with Slee and Allan's (2001) notion that inclusion is a "social movement against educational exclusion" (p. 177). While not all the chapter authors *do* discourse analysis, they do draw our attention to different discourses and how they conflate to include and exclude. Cognisance of our own need to explore these processes allows us to challenge others to do the same, and to work in the interests of current and future policy and inclusive practices.

Overview of this book

Through their writing up of new—or engagement with existing—research and scholarship, the authors (including ourselves) in this book illuminate unjust and just practices, equity, diversity and difference within early childhood education settings. All authors take the position that all members of these settings have the right to fully participate in environments that are, at the very least, welcoming of them and, at most, embracing of their full participation. The authors also acknowledge that creating conditions for inclusion is work that is rewarding and challenging. By sharing ideas, strategies and approaches likely to guide each of us towards discussing and closely examining our values, attitudes and practices, the authors hope that these pages offer early-years teachers and policy makers ideas on how to implement deeper, more meaningful, inclusive and collaborative early childhood practices for now and in the years ahead.

In the first of the contributing authors' chapters (Chapter 2), Sonja Macfarlane and Angus Macfarlane provide us with a new conceptual framework for culturally responsive and inclusive pedagogy in early childhood education. The chapter draws our attention to the right, embedded in law, that all tamariki and their whānau have to participate in early childhood education that is of value and meaning to them. While asserting that there has been a traditional emphasis in Aotearoa New Zealand on instructional and managerial strategies for inclusive education, the authors also remind us that such work has largely occurred at the expense of culture. Sonja and Angus's model is therefore one which shows us that the intricacies of culture are central to any discourse advancing quality and inclusive teaching.

In Chapter 3, Nicola Surtees discusses family diversity. She examines how concepts and practices in early childhood education frequently privilege and construct the orthodox nuclear family as the "norm". Her troubling of the taken-for-granted primacy of heterosexual two-parent family models covers such considerations as legal relationships between parents, legal and biogenetic relationships between parents and tamariki, and co-residence as a benchmark for families. Nicola also draws on the multiple realities of three family constellations led by lesbians and gay men. This highlights changing forms of intimacy and care in the 21st century. She argues that kaiako have a responsibility to attend to such changes. They must then assume diversity in all families they encounter. The chapter concludes by offering us the concept of kinship as a broad framework and resource from which to gain understanding and progress inclusion.

Richard Manning draws on his personal experiences as a Pākehā father to a son who was "taught" a famous Ngāti Toa Rangatira haka at a Christchurch early childhood education centre. In Chapter 4, Richard argues for place-based education that builds community in early childhood education. From his chapter we learn about the histories of the haka in question. Its use in an early childhood centre within the rohe (territory) of Ngāi Tūāhuriri (a hapū of the Ngāi Tahu iwi) is significant to different community members for very different reasons. Richard suggests how early childhood kaiako might engage with local whānau, hapū and iwi to gain the benefit of their local place-based knowledge. This approach, Richard argues, gives meaningful effect to the provisions of Te Tiriti o Waitangi and the United Nations Convention on the Rights of Indigenous Peoples (2007). It involves practices that are consultative and based on open and respectful relations and interactions.

In their chapter (Chapter 5) on the intersection between child and family poverty and access to early childhood education, Glynne Mackey and Colleen Lockie explore the idea that bringing the precepts of citizenship into the care and education of young children favours social justice and equity, and therefore inclusion. Recognising the multiple and disadvantaging impacts of impoverishment on tamariki and whānau, Glynne and Colleen argue that early childhood settings can help ameliorate these influences in the lives of children and families. When early childhood centres actively support children and families to engage in decision making, and thereby strengthen their capacity to take agency in matters that affect them, they contribute to building sustainable and democratic learning communities. The chapter culminates in a discussion of how infants, toddlers and young children within early-years settings can be empowered to contribute as active participants.

In their critical examination of culture in early childhood education (Chapter 6), Gina Colvin, Darcey Dachyshyn and Jo Togiaso deconstruct and reconceptualise several axiomatic and normative ways of being in the world. The authors claim that culture—the extremely complex intergenerational transmission of ideas, beliefs and values—is inextricably linked to sociocultural/historical contexts, and they discuss its significance in the ongoing construction of identity. Premising early childhood settings as colonised spaces, Gina, Darcey and Jo question the dominance of Eurocentric pedagogy and associated power and privilege. They contend that questioning allows us to open up early childhood spaces to other ways of knowing and being. However, the authors caution that if inclusive education is to become a reality, such questioning must be accompanied by a greater sense of humility and self-critique by teachers and policy makers alike.

Arguing against the idea that there is an essential or proper way to be boy- or man-friendly, Alex Gunn explores in her chapter (Chapter 7) the contemporary construction of disadvantage in relation to boys and men in Aotearoa New Zealand early childhood education. In querying the notion that boys need special pedagogies if they are to succeed, Alex also questions the notion of disadvantage as it has been applied to schooling and early childhood education through the recent deployment of discourses of "boys' underachievement", the "feminised workforce", and "marginalised men". Intentionally writing to point out the ways such discourses construct men, boys, women and girls in early childhood education, she unsettles dominant discourses and frames difference as positive. She also reorients thinking away from the notion that early childhood education poses problems for boys and men towards the question of what is fair for different boys, men, girls and women in our field.

Bradley Hannigan's chapter (Chapter 8) draws attention to and investigates the absence of religion in many early childhood centres and services in Aotearoa New Zealand. Arguing that early childhood educational policy and practice are premised on cultural inclusion, Bradley observes that a broader secular approach in contemporary social institutions, particularly education, has consequences for inclusion, diversity and difference. Perceiving religion and culture as inseparable for some, Bradley questions whether we can be said to be practising inclusivity if we obscure children's and families' religious affiliations from view. Bradley reasons that if inclusion is to be taken seriously in Aotearoa New Zealand, then ways must be found to include religious cultures and the religious components of children's culture in our early childhood settings.

The authors of Chapter 9 challenge readers to think about the key factors that contribute to inclusive (or otherwise) early childhood education for children with disabilities and their families. Di Gordon-Burns, Kerry Purdue, Benita Rarere-Briggs, Robyn Stark and Karen Turnock use research and literature to highlight different perspectives on disability. More specifically, they use this material as a basis from which to discuss the kinds of cultures, policies, practices and organisational structures that can lead to an enjoyable and beneficial early-years education for tamariki with disabilities and their whānau. While determinants discussed in this chapter are not intended as a design blueprint, the authors hope that these will guide dialogue about how the issues, challenges and tensions associated with ensuring rights for these children and their families might be addressed and overcome.

The book's final chapter (Chapter 10) summarises and overviews the main themes emerging from the eight contributing chapters. In it, we (Di, Alex, Kerry and Nicola) discuss what has been learned from the contributions of the early childhood scholars in this book. We write about how and why exclusion occurs, about what values and attitudes contribute to inclusion, about the difficulties still facing the realisation of inclusive education, and about engaging in cultural politics for change. We end the chapter by reflecting on and offering a challenge for the future. In particular, we emphasise that change for inclusion has to be advanced at the political, early childhood centre and personal levels if Aotearoa New Zealand is to fully dismantle exclusion and provide a fair, just and democratic education for all. As Slee (2011, p. 176) points out, this task, in itself, "condemns or privileges us to a life of vigilance. All must share in this and this will create difficulty, struggle, tension and new productive relationships. Are we capable? Not alone, we're not."

He matakahi maire.

With a wedge made of maire, a strong and hard wood, it is possible to fell large trees.

(whakataukī/Māori proverb)

References

Allan, J. (Ed.). (2003). *Inclusion, participation and democracy: What is the purpose?* Dordrecht, The Netherlands: Kluwer Academic Publishers.

Allan, J. (2008). *Rethinking inclusive education: The philosophers of difference in practice*. Dordrecht, The Netherlands: Springer.

Ball, S. (1990). *Politics and policy making in education: Explorations in policy sociology*. London, UK: Routledge.

Ballard, K. (Ed.). (1999). *Inclusive education: International voices on disability and justice*. London, UK: Falmer Press.

Bird, L., & Drewery, W. (2004). *Human development in Aotearoa: A journey through life* (2nd ed.). Sydney, NSW, and Auckland: McGraw Hill.

Booth, T., Ainscow, M., & Kingston, D. (2006). *Index for inclusion: Developing play, learning and participation in early years and childcare*. Manchester, UK: Centre for Studies on Inclusive Education.

Booth, T., Nes, K., & Stromstad, M. (Eds.). (2003). *Developing inclusive teacher education*. London, UK: RoutledgeFalmer.

Brennan, M. (2007). A culture of tenderness: Teachers' socialisation practices in group care settings. *European Early Childhood Education Research Journal, 15*(1), 137–146.

Burr, V. (1995). *An introduction to social constructionism*. London, UK: Routledge.

Carr, M., Smith, A. B., Duncan, J., Jones, C., Lee, W., & Marshall, K. (2009). *Learning in the making: Disposition and design in early education*. Rotterdam, The Netherlands: Sense Publishers.

Edwards, S., & Nuttall, J. (Eds.). (2009). *Professional learning in early childhood settings*. Rotterdam, The Netherlands, & Taipei, Taiwan: Sense Publishers.

Fleer, M., Edwards, S., Hammer, M., Kennedy, A., Ridgway, A., Robbins, J., & Surman, L. (2006). *Early childhood learning communities: Sociocultural research in practice*. Frenchs Forest, NSW: Pearson Education Australia.

Foucault, M. (1977). *Discipline and punish: The birth of the prison*. London, UK: Penguin.

Gergen, K. (1999). *An invitation to social construction*. London, UK: Sage Publications.

Gunn, A. C. (2008). *Heteronormativity and early childhood education: Social justice and some puzzling queries*. Unpublished doctoral thesis, University of Waikato.

Gunn, A. C., Child, C., Madden, B., Purdue, K., Surtees, N., Thurlow, B., et al. (2004). Building inclusive communities in early childhood education: Diverse perspectives from Aotearoa/New Zealand. *Contemporary Issues in Early Childhood, 5*(3), 293–308.

Hannigan, B. (2010). *Structural dissonance, enacted hope and initial early childhood teacher education in Aotearoa/New Zealand*. Unpublished doctoral thesis, Victoria University of Wellington.

Jordan, B. (2003). *Professional development making a difference for children: Co-constructing understandings in early childhood centres*. Unpublished doctoral thesis, Massey University.

Keesing-Styles, L., & Hedges, H. (Eds.). (2007). *Theorising early childhood practice: Emerging dialogues*. Castle Hill, NSW: Pademelon Press.

Lave, J., & Wenger, E. (1991). *Situated learning: Legitimate peripheral participation*. Cambridge, UK: Cambridge University Press.

Macartney, B. (2011). *Disabled by the discourse: Two families' narratives of inclusion, exclusion and resistance in education*. Unpublished doctoral thesis, University of Canterbury.

Miller, F., & Katz, J. (2002). *The inclusion breakthrough: Unleashing the real power of diversity*. San Francisco, CA: Berrett-Koehler Publishers.

Minister for Disability Issues. (2001). *New Zealand disability strategy: Making a world of difference—Whakanui oranga*. Wellington: Ministry of Health.

Ministry of Education. (1990). Statement of desirable objectives and practices (DOPs) for chartered early childhood services in New Zealand. *Education Gazette, 69*(23) [special insert].

Ministry of Education. (1996a). Revised statement of desirable objectives and practices (DOPs) for chartered early childhood services in New Zealand. *Education Gazette, 139*(4), 3349–3550.

Ministry of Education. (1996b). *Te whāriki: He whāriki mātauranga mō ngā mokopuna o Aotearoa: Early childhood curriculum.* Wellington: Learning Media.

Ministry of Education. (1998). *Quality in action: Te mahi whai hua: Implementing the revised statement of desirable objectives and practices in New Zealand early childhood services.* Wellington: Learning Media.

Ministry of Education. (2002). *Ngā huarahi arataki: Pathways to the future: A 10-year strategic plan for early childhood education.* Wellington: Learning Media.

Ministry of Education. (2004/09). *Kei tua o te pae: Assessment for learning: Early childhood exemplars.* Wellington: Learning Media.

Ministry of Education. (2007). *The New Zealand curriculum.* Wellington: Author.

Ministry of Education. (2008). *Licensing criteria for early childhood education and care centres 2008 and the Early Childhood Education Curriculum Framework.* Wellington: Ministry of Education.

Ministry of Education. (2009a). *Ka hikitia—Managing for success: The Māori Education Strategy 2008–2012.* Wellington: Author.

Ministry of Education. (2009b). *The Pasifika Education Plan 2008–2012.* Wellington: Author.

Ministry of Education. (2010). *Success for all: Every school, every child.* Wellington: Author.

Moss, P. (2010). We cannot continue as we are: The educator in an education for survival. *Contemporary Issues in Early Childhood, 11*(1), 8–19.

Nuttall, J. (Ed.). (2003). *Weaving Te Whāriki: New Zealand's early childhood curriculum document in theory and practice.* Wellington: New Zealand Council for Educational Research.

Purdue, K. (2004). *Inclusion and exclusion in early childhood education: Three case studies.* Unpublished doctoral thesis, University of Otago.

Purdue, K., Gordon-Burns, D., Gunn, A., Madden, B., & Surtees, N. (2009). Supporting inclusion in early childhood settings: Some possibilities and problems for teacher education. *International Journal of Inclusive Education, 13*(8), 805–815.

Robinson, K., & Jones-Diaz, C. (2005). *Diversity and difference in early childhood education.* Maidenhead, UK: Open University Press.

Slee, R. (2011). *The irregular school: Exclusion, schooling and inclusive education.* London, UK: Routledge.

Slee, R., & Allan, J. (2001). Excluding the included: A reconsideration of inclusive education. *International Studies in Sociology of Education, 11*(2), 173–191.

Surtees, N. (2006). *Sexualities matter in early childhood education: The management of children/bodies and their unsettling desires.* Unpublished master's thesis, Christchurch College of Education.

Surtees, N., & Gunn, A. C. (2010). (Re)marking heteronormativity: Resisting practices in early childhood education contexts. *Australasian Journal of Early Childhood, 35*(1), 42–47.

Terreni, L., Gunn, A., Kelly, J., & Surtees, N. (2010). In and out of the closet: Successes and challenges experienced by gay- and lesbian-headed families in their interactions with the education system in New Zealand. In V. Green & S. Cherrington (Eds.), *Delving into diversity: An international exploration of issues of diversity in education* (pp. 151–161). New York, NY: Nova Science Publishers.

Thomas, G., & Loxley, A. (2001). *Deconstructing special education and constructing inclusion.* Buckingham, UK: Open University Press.

Walden, C. (2011). *Monopoly games in the nursery: Community, inequalities and early childhood education.* Auckland: Salvation Army Social Policy and Parliamentary Unit.

CHAPTER 2

Diversity and inclusion in early childhood education: A bicultural approach to engaging Māori potential

Sonja L. Macfarlane and Angus H. Macfarlane

Introduction

The early years are crucial in the life of a child. Evidence has continued to mount in support of this fact, particularly over the past decade in Aotearoa New Zealand. Although early childhood is not encompassed within the "compulsory" sector of education in this country, all tamariki and their whānau are entitled to access early childhood education if they so choose. This entitlement is not only enshrined in government legislation, but is actively promoted and targeted within key education documents as an invaluable early step in the education pathway of a child. Growth in the early childhood arena has been rapid within our society over the past few years, such that many facilities now offer services, and enrolments continue to rise steadily.

This development, in association with varying perspectives on early childhood development, learning, language acquisition, socialisation and pedagogy, has prompted extensive discussion, debate and inquiry about the quality and efficacy of early childhood provision. This is especially so for finding out what provision works best and why. As a corollary, the role of early childhood kaiako appears to be broadening into domains once deemed outside the scope of responsibility of these practitioners. One such domain is that of cultural responsiveness.

Because the intricacies of culture are central to current discourses on quality teaching, we draw together in this chapter theory and research findings to show how cultural responsiveness has developed as a concept, how it has added to conversations about diversity, and how it might be manifested in practice within the day-to-day work of early childhood teachers. The central feature of this chapter is an early-childhood-specific framework that discerning practitioners can use when working with tamariki Māori and their whānau.

The importance of the foundational years

If children are to learn and to interact successfully throughout their schooling and beyond, it is essential that they develop strong foundations in their early years. According to Claxton and Carr (2004), successful learning and socialisation enables children to remain engaged, develop positive self-efficacy and reach their potential as they progress through the education system. Claxton and Carr's claim is supported by a considerable amount of evidence which clearly indicates that high-quality interactions in early childhood care and education settings have enduring benefits for children as they continue to learn and grow (see, for example, Desforges & Abouchaar, 2003; Tahuri, 2005; Wylie & Hipkins, 2006).

More specifically, this body of work shows that these interactions lay the foundations on which children construct many of their social, cultural, psychological, physical and educational habits and beliefs. Related research conducted in Aotearoa New Zealand shows that the availability of culturally responsive early childhood education helps determine whether parents of tamariki Māori choose to participate in early childhood education (ERO, 2010; Rameka, 2003; Tahuri, 2005). These findings must surely require all early childhood educators to reflect on and interrogate the what, why, how and who of their teaching theory and praxis—to consider *what* is included in the curriculum, *why* it is important, *how* it is constructed and operationalised, and *who* it will benefit.

The national mainstream context of diversity in early childhood education

Improving educational outcomes for Māori learners is a key priority for the education sector. Current education strategies focus on improving the ways in which the education system enables Māori learners to achieve better outcomes and to realise their potential (Ministry of Education, 2008). Within that wider sector, early childhood services have a key role to play in building the strong learning foundations that enable young children to develop as competent and confident learners. *Ka Hikitia*, the Ministry of Education's Māori education strategy for the years 2008 to 2012, firmly established two interrelated priorities for action:

- ensuring that Māori tamariki participate in "quality early childhood education"
- strengthening the participation of Māori whānau in their children's learning (Ministry of Education, 2008, p. 21).

Most Māori children (76 percent) who participate in early childhood education do so in mainstream settings (Ministry of Education, 2010). A requirement for early childhood education services to be responsive to the needs of Māori children and their whānau is by no means new. The Ministry of Education outlined this obligation in 2002 in its 10-year strategic plan for early childhood education (2001–2010):

[Because] many Māori children attend mainstream ECE [early childhood education] services, ensuring these services are responsive to their needs and those of their whānau is a priority. (Ministry of Education, 2002, p. 10)

In 2010, Aotearoa New Zealand's Education Review Office (ERO) reported on the quality of the provision of education and care for Māori children in 576 early childhood services. The evaluation concentrated on the extent to which these services:

- responded to the aspirations and expectations of parents and whānau of tamariki Māori
- focused on realising the potential of Māori children to become competent and confident learners.

The 2010 evaluation confirmed the findings of an earlier ERO-conducted pilot study of Māori children in early childhood settings (ERO, 2008). Both studies found that the services ERO evaluated:

- said they "treated all children the same" and lacked strategies that focused on Māori children as learners
- included statements about values, beliefs and intentions in centre documentation that were not evident in practice
- did not use effective processes to find out about the aspirations of parents and whānau of tamariki Māori
- lacked adequate self-review processes to evaluate the effectiveness of their provision for Māori children.

The results of these two studies strongly suggest that a fundamental challenge for early childhood managers and kaiako is to understand, review and develop processes that enable them to listen to, respect and respond to the aspirations and expectations of Māori whānau in authentic ways. The 2010 ERO review also found that, despite most early childhood services having processes for consulting and communicating with Māori whānau, fewer than half (41 percent) were using such processes to identify and respond to the aspirations and expectations of Māori families. A second concern centred on the quality and relevance of the curriculum. The ERO found that almost two-thirds (65 percent) of the early childhood services reviewed had implemented what they considered to be a bicultural curriculum. However, the quality and relevance of this was variable. Managers and teachers did not appear to fully recognise the importance of acknowledging Māori children's cultural identity and heritage (see also, in this regard, Rameka, 2003).

Ka Hikitia and *Te Whāriki*: A dual strategic focus on the early years

Ka Hikitia (Ministry of Education, 2008) urges Aotearoa New Zealand's education system to fit the student rather than requiring the student to fit the education system. Such an approach requires children, families, whānau, hapū, iwi, educators, communities and government to work together in partnership and to learn from one another. This perspective is fundamental to the principles of inclusive practice, whereby children of all abilities are embraced for their uniqueness, and where families are central to learning interactions (Gordon-Burns, Purdue, Rarere-Briggs, Stark, & Turnock, 2010; Margrain, 2010).

The early childhood curriculum, *Te Whāriki* (Ministry of Education, 1996), provides the framework for learning in early childhood education settings. Like *Ka Hikitia*, *Te Whāriki* supports the concept of ako—effective teaching and learning (pedagogy) based on reciprocal relationships and incorporating the people and contexts of children's wider lives. The concept of ako also embraces two other important notions. Firstly, *culture counts*. Culture counts is about knowing, respecting and valuing who students are and where they come from, and then building on what they bring with them. Second, is the value of *productive relationships*. The focus here is on children, families, whānau, hapū, iwi and kaiako sharing knowledge and expertise with one another to produce enhanced and shared outcomes.

As the early childhood education curriculum framework, *Te Whāriki* provides a robust rationale and an inherent expectation that mainstream early childhood services will put a bicultural curriculum in place. This curriculum is one that embodies the language, culture and values of both Māori and Pākehā and is ultimately responsive to the principles of Te Tiriti o Waitangi. Being responsive to the Treaty principles requires early childhood services to consider how they incorporate the principles of partnership, protection and participation within theory, praxis and relationships (Bishop & Glynn, 1999). ERO (2010) found that most services were incorporating a degree of te reo Māori and including some practices consistent with tikanga Māori. However, it was obvious that incorporating Māori perspectives into planning, assessment and evaluation processes was still a challenge for many early childhood services.

Thus, not all early childhood education services have managers and kaiako who are competent in te reo Māori. Not all understand and acknowledge Te Tiriti o Waitangi and Māori cultural values. Nor do they all work in partnership with whānau and the wider Māori community to provide high-quality education for Māori children. This situation highlights the need for early childhood managers and educators to undergo ongoing professional development focused on the importance of cultural responsiveness to Māori.

The theoretical base of *Te Whāriki* is situated within sociocultural education theory (Rogoff, 1990, 1995, 1998; Wertsch, 1991). We consider that referencing this theory provides a way forward for early childhood practitioners. A sociocultural perspective recognises that individuals can be understood only in relation to their social and cultural context. Rather than focusing on a child's behaviour (the traditional individualistic model), this understanding acknowledges that sociocultural activity is the unit of analysis. Attention is given

to the "structure of the cultural/historical activities in which …
[children] participate" (Rogoff, 1998, p. 715) and to which they
contribute. The sociocultural perspective thus recognises that no
child is independent of ethnicity, culture, whakapapa and language.
Te Whāriki positions tamariki within their sociocultural context of
family and community and recognises the centrality of relationships
and culture to children's wellbeing, identity and learning (Ministry
of Education, 1996).

The difficulties of implementing sociocultural teaching practices
in early childhood services arise when such practices are poorly
understood by teachers and are inconsistent with traditional practices
in early childhood centres (Cullen, 2003). Cullen states that many
teachers seem constrained by the belief that if children are able to
express themselves through play, then their culture will be respected.
This view fails to recognise that play itself is a culturally bound
construct that may not be reflected in the communities of practice
in which children's lives are embedded (Fleer, 2001).

A culturally responsive framework for early childhood education

Within Aotearoa New Zealand, any culturally responsive pedagogical
framework must reflect the nation's bicultural heritage. This heritage
is a significant aspect of the unique sociocultural context that exists
in our country. Much of the focus of policy making in education has
emanated out of the bicultural relationship between Māori (as the
indigenous people) and Pākehā (descendants of the British settlers).
This relationship is enshrined in our nation's founding document,
Te Tiriti o Waitangi, signed by representatives of the two peoples
in 1840. The agreement between the two Treaty partners on the
governance and organisation of our nation is acknowledged in key
legislative (including educational) documents, such as *Te Whāriki*
and *Ka Hikitia*.

Te Whāriki states that "In early childhood education settings, all children should be given the opportunity to develop knowledge and an understanding of the cultural heritages of both partners of Te Tiriti o Waitangi" (p. 9), while *Ka Hikitia* positions "The Treaty of Waitangi ... [as] a valued relationship management tool, symbolic of our past and central to our future" (p. 9). Another document prepared by the Ministry of Education (2006), *Specialist Service Standards*, requires the professional practice of specialists working with babies, children and young people (i.e., 0 to 20 years of age) who have special education needs to reflect standards "developed through a process that reflects the principles of Te Tiriti o Waitangi" (p. 6).

Within an educational context, understanding how the Treaty affects theory and praxis is essential if services are to reflect a bicultural ethos, and to be culturally responsive to tamariki Māori and their whānau. Certainly, the clear intentions of *Te Whāriki, Ka Hikitia* and *Specialist Service Standards* make it a natural progression to consider how Te Tiriti o Waitangi might be operationalised as a practice framework for early childhood teachers.

Te Pikinga ki Runga (Macfarlane & Macfarlane, 2008) is a planning framework intended to guide education professionals in their interactions when working with Māori tamariki and their whānau. The framework (set out in its most recent form in Figure 1) was originally developed to facilitate work with Māori ākonga exhibiting severe and challenging behaviours in education settings which placed them at risk of educational underachievement—or even failure. However, it has become increasingly clear that education practitioners (including early childhood kaiako) can use it for a range of purposes and in various contexts.

We stress that the framework is not a recipe for "fixing" the particular situation or individual. Rather, the intention behind it is to raise possibilities for Māori children as they grapple with learning, socialisation, peer interactions and—in some cases—the very essence of their own identity. In response to these realities, we decided, when developing the framework, that the teaching pedagogy resulting from its application should be guided by three fundamental human rights principles, briefly mentioned earlier, each of which sits at the very heart of our bicultural society in Aotearoa New Zealand—Te Tiriti o Waitangi. They are *partnership*, *protection* and *participation*.

Principles that count

PRINCIPLE ONE: Partnership—partnering and engaging with whānau

Whānau is at the core of the Treaty principle of partnership. Research, both national and international, highlights the critical importance of education professionals building and maintaining positive relationships with whānau and caregivers. In Aotearoa New Zealand, we now recognise that effective engagement and consultation with whānau (and the cultural community) is a crucial component of educational decision making, and of education outcomes achieved by ākonga (Bevan-Brown, 2001, 2003; Kingi & Durie, 2000; Macfarlane, 2005).

But what does effective partnering look like? What are the key components? Glynn, Berryman, Walker, Reweti and O'Brien (2001) employ a "life partnership analogy". To show that what we know and understand about conducting personal partnerships in life can guide us in establishing effective working partnerships with others. The analogy highlights the destructive outcomes that can occur within relationships should one partner hold a far more powerful and dominant position than the other. Effective partnering with whānau therefore needs to consider how power is shared and balanced (Bishop & Glynn, 1999). Te Pikinga ki Runga includes a range of dimensions that need to be addressed when responding to the Treaty principle of partnership. These are set out under the heading Huakina Mai (opening doorways) in Figure 1.

Figure 1: Te Pikinga ki Runga (Copyright © 2008, 2011 Sonja and Angus Macfarlane)

Part A: Raising the Possibilities

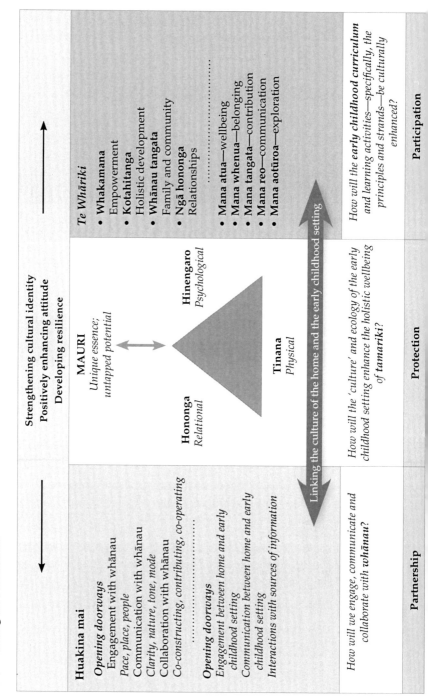

Part B: Te Hua—protecting the wellbeing of tamariki ... reflective questions to inform theory and praxis

Domains

	Hononga (Relational aspects)	Hinengaro (Psychological aspects)	Tinana (Physical aspects)	Mauri (Unique essence)
Dimensions	Whānau — *Interdependence and connectedness*	Motivation — *Inspiration and drive*	Demeanour — *Appearance and body language*	Cultural identity — *Pride and security*
	Whenua — *Kinship and belonging*	Emotions — *Thoughts and feelings*	Energy levels — *Alertness and zeal*	Attitude and spirit — *Manner and disposition*
	Friendships — *Co-operation and empathy*	Cognition — *Learning and understanding*	Physical safety — *Respect for self and others*	Potential — *Courage and confidence*

Domain	Reflective questions
HONONGA Relational aspects ... within the whānau and with others *Consider how the programme plan will support and strengthen social relationships*	How strong are relationships between tamariki and whānau ... their connectedness to their whānau? How strong are their connections to/relationships with others (whānau whānui, hapū, iwi ...)? How is their position in their whānau being acknowledged (i.e., the eldest, youngest, only son/daughter ...)? How strong are their connections to/relationships with places (papakāinga, marae, whenua ...)? Whānau whānui: how might wider whānau contribute or feature? How strong (positive) are the relationships between tamariki and key others (peers, teachers ...)?
HINENGARO Psychological aspects ... thoughts and feelings, learning *Consider how the programme plan will uplift and strengthen the thoughts and feelings*	What are the things that inspire and motivate each tamaiti? How do tamariki display/express their emotions (verbally, non-verbally)? How respectful are they of others' thoughts and feelings? Do they understand what others are communicating to them? How is all this affecting their engagement/participation in activities at the early childhood setting? How is all this affecting their learning and achievement?
TINANA Physical aspects ... demeanour, physical health and wellbeing *Consider how the programme plan will enhance physical health and wellbeing*	How is their āhua (their demeanour appearance)—how does each tamaiti 'look'? What messages might tamariki be expressing with their body language? What are their energy levels like? How alert are they? Are others respecting the personal space of each tamaiti? Are these tamariki respecting the personal space of others?
MAURI Unique essence ... cultural identity, attitude, potential *Consider how the programme plan will strengthen and enhance identity and overall wellbeing*	How is the cultural identity of tamariki being supported and strengthened by others (early childhood setting, peers)? How is meaning derived from the name of each tamaiti? How is the self-concept of each tamaiti affecting his or her attitude (e.g., responses to others, manner, outlook)? How might the attitude/spirit (their mana) of tamariki be enhanced and uplifted? What opportunities are being provided which enable tamariki to make positive choices? How can tamariki be supported to build their confidence and strengthen their resilience?

PRINCIPLE TWO: Protection—protecting and enhancing children's wellbeing, identity and self-concept

Tamariki are at the heart of the Treaty principle of protection. This principle acknowledges the importance of protecting and enhancing children's self-concept and cultural identity by utilising strengths-based and holistic approaches to overall health and wellbeing. *Ka Hikitia* (Ministry of Education, 2008) urges moving away from a focus on deficit towards a focus on potential for those seeking to be responsive to Māori children. This strategic document thus stresses the importance of "realising Māori potential" by emphasising strengths.

A range of frameworks that have this focus are currently available for practitioners working with Māori in both educational and health settings. These frameworks include:

- James Irwin's (1984) triangle, encompassing the elements of mind, body, and spirit
- Rose Pere's (1991) framework, *Te Wheke*
- Mason Durie's (1994) *Te Whare Tapa Whā*
- Mason Durie's (1999) *Te Pae Mahutonga*.

Research undertaken by Durie (1998) supports the belief that Māori who are more secure in their own cultural identity and self-concept have higher educational aspirations and outcomes than those who are less secure. Tajfel and Turner (1986) describe self-concept as having two key components. The first component is *personal identity*, which covers such characteristics as one's own particular talents or abilities. The second is *social identity*, which emanates out of our own awareness of personal membership in a particular social group, and out of the emotional significance that we each place on our own involvement in that group (Tajfel, 1981).

When developing Te Pikinga ki Runga, we drew on the frameworks and notions developed by Irwin, Pere, Durie, and Tajfel and Turner, to bring four holistic domains to our educational approach to wholeness and wellbeing. One domain was the Māori concept of wairua or spirituality (Durie, 1994). While these frameworks include wairua as a key element, Māori and non-Māori have challenged whether education practitioners have the ability to respond effectively and authentically to this concept within education. After reflection, we decided that three domains—hononga, hinengaro and tinana (relational aspects, psychological aspects and physical aspects)— should comprise the core configuration—that of a triangle—of our framework. We also decided, however, that the framework should offer an encompassing and emanating fourth domain—mana motuhake (self-concept). This fourth, we determined, is integral to—and an outcome of—all four domains working effectively together.

To help practitioners "unpack" the four domains, we broke each one down into three sub-dimensions, resulting in 12 dimensions in total. We refer, with affection, to the dimensions grid within the framework as Te Huia—a name gifted by a kuia who participated in a seminar where we initially shared the thinking behind Te Pikinga ki Runga. For her, the 12 dimensions of the grid represented 12 prized tail feathers from the extinct huia bird. If, she explained, we do not protect or care for these feathers (her metaphor for tamariki), then we risk their "extinction". The Te Huia dimension grid is further supported by a set of reflective prompt questions that practitioners can consider when implementing and putting into practice the Treaty principle of protection.

PRINCIPLE THREE: Participation—enhancing the curriculum to support presence, participation and learning for tamariki

Under this principle, the primary focus is again tamariki, but this time as learners in, members of and contributors to the ecology of the early childhood settings in which they find themselves. This principle is responsive to the various intentions underpinning the principles and strands of *Te Whāriki* (Ministry of Education, 1996)—the vehicles by which early childhood ecology, pedagogy and curriculum are enriched, and child participation and learning therefore ignited (Brewerton, 2004). The principles are *whakamana* (empowerment), *kotahitanga* (holistic development), *whānau tangata* (family and community) and *ngā hononga* (relationships). The strands are Mana Atua (wellbeing), Mana Whenua (belonging), Mana Tangata (contribution), Mana Reo (communication) and Mana Aotūroa (exploration).

According to Rutherford (2004), these interconnected areas of skill and expertise are the essence of successful learning throughout life. The principles and strands of *Te Whāriki* serve the Treaty principle of participation within Te Pikinga ki Runga. They make clear the need for learning environments (context and content) to be inclusive of, and responsive to, the needs of each child (again see Figure 1).

Summary and conclusion

In the field of mainstream educational research and practice, Western theories and knowledge have formed, for many years, the conventional and acceptable sources from which educational theorists, policy makers and kaiako have drawn their ideas and practice. This "mainstream" thinking is endemic in all sectors of the education system in Aotearoa New Zealand, including early childhood education. Many of these sources have been—and still are—adroit and effective in their responsiveness to tamariki Māori and their whānau. However, they have inherent within them the risk of homogenising practice and, thus, potentially marginalising a significant sector of the learner population. This risk is manifested in programmes, activities and relationships that are not sufficiently responsive.

Cultural dimensions within early childhood education services thus regularly pose challenges for many early childhood educators because they are value-laden. Conventional approaches regularly subjugate cultural aspects, because these aspects are perceived as outside "the norm". Educationalists need to go beyond strictly Western and conventional educational approaches by adopting a more culturally grounded approach to their policy and practice. This need is made particularly cogent in Aotearoa New Zealand by the bicultural partnership between Māori and Pākehā under Te Tiriti o Waitangi. For mainstream early childhood education services, this means delving into Māori concepts, beliefs and values to explore the thinking that characterises models such as *Te Whāriki, Te Wheke* and *Te Whare Tapa Whā*. The aim of this process, in turn, is to derive meanings that translate into culturally appropriate early childhood praxis.

This said, educational stakeholders in Aotearoa New Zealand appear to have become increasingly aware that the dominant culture determines and provides the professional delivery of education, even though the minority culture increasingly provides the students. The educational framework that we have developed, Te Pikinga ki Runga, provides a means of "capturing" and building on this growing awareness. Because Te Pikinga ki Runga draws from the richness of Māori literature, and because it incorporates the "voices" of Māori practitioners and researchers, it encourages discerning early childhood teachers to convert culturally responsive theory into practice. The framework propounds the idea that the social and cultural nuances that are seen in one culture may also be found in another. Yet it also reminds us that these nuances may bear a completely different significance in each.

Providing quality and culturally responsive early childhood education services for Māori children and their whānau has tested educators for many years. The challenge is compounded by many factors, not the least of which is the dearth of trained professionals within the workforce who are Māori. Te Pikinga ki Runga is a response to this challenge. Underpinned by the principles of Te Tiriti o Waitangi, appreciative of the impact of engaging with the home environment, responsive to the holistic wellbeing of tamariki, and cognisant of the early childhood strands that early childhood kaiako wish to promote in early childhood settings, this framework seeks to untangle some intricacies for educators in their work with tamariki Māori—and indeed, with all children and their whānau.

References

Bevan-Brown, J. (2001). Evaluating special educational services for learners from ethnically diverse groups: Getting it right. *Journal of the Association for Persons with Severe Handicaps, 26*, 138–147.

Bevan-Brown, J. (2003). *The cultural self-review: Providing culturally effective, inclusive education for Māori learners.* Wellington: New Zealand Council for Educational Research.

Bishop, R., & Glynn, T. (1999). *Culture counts: Changing power relations in education.* Palmerston North: Dunmore Press.

Brewerton, M. (2004). *Reframing the essential skills: Implications of the OECD defining and selecting key competencies project.* Wellington: Ministry of Education.

Claxton, G., & Carr, M. (2004). A framework for teaching learning: Learning dispositions. *Early Years International Journal of Research and Development, 24*(1) 87–97.

Cullen, J. (2003). The challenge of *Te Whāriki*: Catalyst for change? In J. Nuttall (Ed.), *Weaving Te Whāriki: New Zealand's early childhood curriculum document in theory and practice* (pp. 269–296). Wellington: New Zealand Council for Educational Research.

Desforges, C., & Abouchaar, A. (2003). *The impact of parental involvement, parental support and family education on pupil achievement and adjustment: A literature review* Nottingham, UK: DfES Publications. Retrieved from http://www.bgfl.org/bgfl/custom/files_ uploaded/uploaded _resources/18617/Desforges.pdf

Durie, M. H. (1994). *Whaiora: Māori health development.* Auckland: Oxford University Press.

Durie, M. H. (1998). *Te mana te kawanatanga: The politics of Māori sovereignty.* Auckland: Oxford University Press.

Durie, M. H. (1999). Te Pae Mahutonga: A model for Māori health promotion. *Health Promotion Forum of New Zealand Newsletter, 49*, 2–5.

ERO (Education Review Office). (2008). *Māori children in early childhood: A pilot study.* Wellington: Author.

ERO (Education Review Office). (2010). *Success for Māori in early childhood services.* Wellington: Author.

Fleer, M., (2001). *An early childhood research agenda: Voices from the field.* Canberra, ACT: Department of Education, Training and Youth Affairs.

Glynn, T., Berryman, M., Walker, R., Reweti, M., & O'Brien, K. (2001, July). *Partnerships with indigenous people: Modifying the cultural mainstream.* Keynote address at the Partnerships in Education Psychology Conference, Brisbane, Australia.

Gordon-Burns, D., Purdue, K., Rarere-Briggs, B., Stark, R., & Turnock, K. (2010). Quality inclusive early childhood education for children with disabilities and their families: Learning from research. *International Journal of Equity and Innovation in Early Childhood, 8*(1), 53–68.

Irwin, J. (1984). *An introduction to Māori religion.* Adelaide, SA: Australian Association for the Study of Religions.

Kingi, T. K., & Durie, M. H. (2000). *Hua oranga: A Māori measure of mental health outcomes.* Palmerston North: School of Māori Studies, Massey University.

Macfarlane, A. (2005). Inclusion and Māori ecologies: An educultural approach. In D. Fraser, R. Moltzen, & K. Ryba. (Eds.), *Learners with special needs in Aotearoa New Zealand* (3rd ed., pp. 77–98), Melbourne, VIC: Thomson Dunmore Press.

Macfarlane, S., & Macfarlane, A. (2008). *Te Pikinga ki Runga: Raising possibilities: A culturally responsive framework for working with Māori learners and whānau.* Wellington: Ministry of Education, Special Education.

Margrain, V. (2010). Parent–teacher partnership for gifted early readers in New Zealand. *International Journal about Parents in Education, 4*(1), 39–48.

Ministry of Education. (1996). *Te whāriki: He whāriki mātauranga mō ngā mokopuna o Aotearoa: Early childhood curriculum.* Wellington: Learning Media.

Ministry of Education. (2002). *Pathways to the future: Ngā huarahi arataki: A 10-year strategic plan for early childhood education.* Wellington: Author.

Ministry of Education. (2008). *Ka hikitia: Managing for success.* Wellington: Author.

Ministry of Education. (2010). *Ngā haeata mātauranga: The annual report on Māori education.* Wellington: Author.

Ministry of Education. (2006). *Specialist service standards.* Wellington: Ministry of Education.

Pere, R. (1991). *Te Wheke: A celebration of ultimate wisdom.* Gisborne: Ao Ako.

Rameka, L. (2003, January). *Cultural values and understandings as quality outcomes for early childhood.* Paper presented at the Reconceptualising Early Childhood Education Conference, Tempe, Arizona, USA.

Rogoff, B. (1990). *Apprenticeship in thinking: Cognitive development in social context.* New York, NY: Oxford University Press.

Rogoff, B. (1995). Observing socio-cultural activity on three planes: Participatory appropriation, guided participation and apprenticeship. In J. Wertsch, P. Del Riot, & A. Alvirez (Eds.), *Socio-cultural studies of the mind* (pp. 139–164). New York, NY: Cambridge University Press.

Rogoff, B. (1998). Cognition as a collaborative process. In D. Kuhn & R. Siegler (Eds.), *Handbook of child psychology: Volume 2: Cognition, perception and language* (5th ed., pp. 679–744). New York, NY: John Wiley.

Rutherford, J. (2004). *Key competencies in the New Zealand curriculum: A snapshot of consultation, December 2004.* Wellington: Ministry of Education.

Tahuri, B. (2005, December). *Weaving links between the community and the school: Kia tika—kia pono.* Paper presented to the New Zealand Association of Research in Education Conference, University of Otago, Dunedin.

Tajfel, H. (1981). *Human groups and social categories: Studies in social psychology.* Cambridge, MA: Cambridge University Press.

Tajfel, H., & Turner, J. C. (1986). The social identity theory of intergroup behaviour. In S. Worchel & W. Austin (Eds), *Psychology of intergroup relations* (2nd ed., pp. 7–24). Chicago, IL: Nelson-Hall.

Wertsch, J. V. (1991). *Voices of the mind: A sociological approach to mediated action.* Cambridge, MA: Cambridge University Press.

Wylie, C., & Hipkins, E. (2006). *Growing independence: Competent students @ 14.* Wellington: Research Division, Ministry of Education.

CHAPTER 3

Families and kinship: Reframing forms of intimacy and care in inclusionary early childhood education settings

Nicola Surtees

Introduction

"Family" is a contested site: ambiguous, powerful and imbued with symbolic significance, concepts of family are important in the lives of adults and children (Morgan, 1996; Silva & Smart, 1999; Smart, 2007; Weeks, Heaphy, & Donovan, 2001). This chapter adopts a critical stance to concepts of family, positioning families as richly diverse, changing and constituted by what they do rather than as a homogeneous ideological construct. As Morgan (1996) states, the family "is not a thing" (p. 11) or a timeless, fixed unit or structure. The family is better understood as sets of family practices or forms of *doing* family, instead of static arrangements or idealised relationships. Specifically focusing on such practices, this chapter draws attention to and makes problematic the taken-for-granted primacy of heterosexual two-parent family forms, legal relationships between parents, legal and biogenetic relationships between parents and children, and co-residence as a benchmark for families.

In Aotearoa New Zealand, legislation and policy (e.g., the Human Rights Act 1993; Ministry of Education, 1996a, 1996b, 1998) support the inclusion of *all* families in early childhood education. Accordingly, early childhood teachers have a responsibility to make sure that the right of all whānau to belong is upheld (Ministry of Education, 1996b). Heteronormative discourses predominating in the field present difficulties for exercising this responsibility. Such discourses serve to constitute nuclear family forms as "proper" family forms through the privileging of heterosexual couples and their legally and biogenetically related tamariki (Surtees & Gunn, 2010). Marked as "normal", such "proper" families obscure those marked as "abnormal" and "improper". These obscured families include, for example, extended families; reconstituted families post-divorce and post-separation that have reconfigured fully or partially independently of ties that are legal or biogenetic (or both); families that have come about through assisted reproduction or adoption practices, where biogenetic connections are not necessarily present; and families parented by lesbians and gay men.

When the language and practices of early childhood kaiako are governed by heteronormative discourses, it can become difficult for teachers to "see" and thus meaningfully include such families. Where this is the case, policy, administrative forms, curriculum experiences, and materials and resources are unlikely to fully support and positively represent varied forms of doing family. Exclusion, for some whānau, may result.

In this chapter I introduce three family constellations[1] led by lesbians and gay men. In exploring the ways their doing of family disrupts the (hetero)norm, I attempt to highlight changing forms of intimacy and care in the 21st century. I suggest that early childhood

---

1 The descriptor "family constellation" is used in this chapter as a means of grouping together those adults who have entered into relationships with one another for the purpose of conceiving children. The adults introduced in the chapter would not necessarily understand their reproductive relationships as "family" ties.

kaiako must respond to such changes in order not only to meet their legislated inclusionary responsibilities, but also to challenge exclusion. I conclude by suggesting that the notion of "kinship" may prove useful as a broad framework for understanding and including diverse families. This is because kinship transcends simplistic categorisation of groups of people based on law, biology, genetics or residency.

Framing the study: Family, kinship and relatedness in the era of assisted reproduction

The qualitative research study that I draw on in this chapter involves a continuing investigation of the planned and actual family relationships of lesbians, gay men and their children. The study is framed by Morgan's (1996) notion of family practices and concepts of kinship and relatedness in the era of assisted reproduction.

Unlike early concepts of kinship, newer concepts of kinship no longer privilege the allegedly natural processes of reproduction over other forms of connectedness. For example, Mason (2008) embraces shifting ideas of who is tied to whom beyond marriage and biogenetics (Edwards, 2000; Smart, 2007; Smart, Neale, & Wade, 2001; Strathern, 1992), suggesting that kinship has "a strong life resonance because it helps us to theorise the kinds of kin relationships that people really engage in" (p. 31). Mason concludes that, for many people, kinship relationships are about "the way they live out *particular* relationships with others through different sets of interpersonal dynamics that are specific to *that* relationship and *that* person" (p. 37, italics in original). Increasingly, kin relationships are understood as personalised, adaptable and based on bonds of affection (Smart et al., 2001), and so are able to encompass various relationships and people. These ideas suggest choice in the claiming of bonds and forms of intimacy and care.

A shift towards choice is noted in studies of the relatedness of reconstituted families that come into being after separation and divorce (see, for example, Fleming, 1999; Smart et al., 2001; Stacey, 1990). Choice has also been explored by Weston (1991) with respect to the relatedness of lesbians and gay men. She emphasises the ways in which the women and men she surveyed chose kin relationships that embraced informal, strong, supportive networks of lovers and friends rather than relationships based on formal structured heterosexual alliances.

Redefinitions of kin relationships and assisted reproduction enhance the possibilities for choice for both heterosexual-led and lesbian- and gay-led whānau. Significantly for lesbians and gay men, assisted reproduction uncouples heterosexual sex and conception (Agigian, 2004; Dempsey, 2005; Mezey, 2008; Weeks et al., 2001). As Weeks et al. state, this happenstance represents "one of the key moments in the history of possibilities for non-heterosexual parenting" (p. 165). While donor insemination and newer reproductive technologies such as ovum retrieval, in-vitro fertilisation and traditional or gestational surrogacy developed as remedies for infertility in heterosexual couples (Wikler & Wikler, 1991), lesbians have practised donor insemination since the 1970s, often with the assistance of gay men (Agigian, 2004; Pollack & Vaughn, 1987; Weeks et al., 2001; Weston, 1993).

Assisted reproduction frequently makes biogenetic connections negotiable and compounds their meanings. Dempsey (2005) describes this as "a by-product of the intervention of third parties in the reproductive processes" (p. 43). Edwards, Franklin, Hirsch, Price, and Strathern (1999) note that the use of third parties as "new procreative actors" (p. 23) can generate separation between biogenetic and social parents. In Fleming's (1999) view, a division occurs between those parents previously thought of as the mother and the father and other people who can claim parenthood. By drawing attention to family relationships "we do not yet have names for" (Silva & Smart, 1999, p. 10), third parties are both critical to and can challenge the family innovation of infertile heterosexual couples and lesbians and gay men alike.

Method

Qualitative research demands the gathering of comprehensive, thoroughly detailed data for in-depth interpretative study (Bogdan & Biklen, 1998; Patton, 2002). The open-ended, semi-structured interview is a useful tool to this end. In the present case, it proved well suited to an exploration of the planned and actual family relationships of lesbians, gay men and their tamariki.

Potential participants offered to be interviewed after seeing national electronic and print media advertising of the study, which specifically targeted lesbian and gay communities. Potential participants were also accessed through snowball sampling in established lesbian and gay networks, where those who expressed interest in the study were invited to recommend others. Snowball sampling is a useful technique for accessing difficult-to-reach interconnected populations (Cohen, Manion, & Morrison, 2000; Neuman, 1997).

These recruitment strategies secured the participation of most adult members of 21 family constellations. These families were ones in which lesbians and gay men (and, in some cases, straight men) planned to conceive and co-parent tamariki together, or to otherwise take up an agreed role of some description with those tamariki, or had already conceived (and given birth to) children and were actively co-parenting together or engaging in an agreed role with them. Diversity was sought across the two participant sets, loosely categorised as either "prospective families" (nine) or "existing families" (twelve), in terms of the number of potential co-parents or actual co-parents, the variety of other roles planned or taken up, and family configurations. Other factors looked for included methods of conception, and the distribution of family members across households.

Open-ended semi-structured interviews were used to produce data from both sets of families. Twenty-seven interviews were conducted over a period of 4 months, with family members interviewed in configurations and settings of their choice. Organising the interviews in this way avoided predetermining who was "in" a family, especially where members were distributed across more than one household. All interviews were recorded and transcribed, and hard copies of the transcriptions were sent to participants with an invitation to add their comments in the interests of creating an accurate recording of the interview.

All interview data were subjected to content analysis. A qualitative data analysis software package (NVivo 9) was used to analyse, code and manage the interview material.

Approval for the study was obtained from the University of Canterbury's Human Ethics Committee. The study has adhered to, and continues to adhere to, the ethical requirements of informed consent, voluntary participation and confidentiality. Provisions for anonymity have also been made to protect the identities of participants and their tamariki. Real names are not used in the study and resulting publications, and, in some cases, identifying information such as the ages and genders of children have also been changed to preserve anonymity.

Diverse family practices: Disrupting the (hetero)norm

This section of the chapter introduces three family constellations led by lesbians and gay men. In foregrounding the diverse family practices of these women and men, I point to the ways their doing of family disrupts the (hetero)norm. They trouble the taken-for-granted primacy of heterosexual two-parent models, legal relationships between parents, legal and biogenetic relationships between parents and children, and co-residence as a benchmark for families. This section also highlights the challenging conditions the women and men faced in their desire for tamariki—conditions less frequently experienced by their heterosexual counterparts. Of particular significance is the finding and establishing of reproductive relationships. Dempsey (2010) describes such a relationship as "a connection made with a person of the other sex necessary for the purposes of having a baby" (p. 1146).

Vivian, Moira, Wilson and Johan

The first family constellation included two sets of couples. Vivian and Moira, the first couple, planned to do family by asking a gay couple to help them conceive and then co-parent a tamaiti. Many lesbians prefer gay men as donors (Donovan, 2000; Ryan-Flood, 2005). Vivian's explanation of why this was important is not atypical:

> It's always been important to us that our donor should be a gay man. In most cases, it's so easy for heterosexual men to be fathers; it's seen as natural. On the other hand, it's almost impossible for a gay man to become a father if he wants to … We genuinely wanted to give a gay man—or, in this case, two—the chance to experience parenthood. It's our small way of trying to redress the unfairness.

Unsettling the taken-for-granted primacy of heterosexual two-parent models, the women's plans for doing family necessitated a long search for the right men with whom to establish a reproductive relationship. Although the search is a common experience for lesbians (Dempsey, 2010; Gunn & Surtees, 2009; Vaccaro, 2010), it was nevertheless challenging for Vivian and Moira. It culminated in the women's introduction over the internet to the second couple, Wilson and Johan. As Moira explained, "We've met through this process. We weren't known to one another previously; it was wanting to have a child that brought us together."

Likening the initial period spent getting to know one another to dating, the couples' "dates" soon included sensitive and potentially fraught discussions about fertility, the mechanics of donor insemination, parenting values, and the significance of legal and biogenetic parent–child relationships—topics less likely to be debated by heterosexual couples. Well versed in the possibilities for legal and biogenetic parent–child relationships, this family constellation illustrates the complexities of these matters for many lesbian- and gay-led families: the presence of a legal tie does not necessarily denote the presence of a biogenetic tie, and vice versa, as is generally assumed in heterosexual-led families.

As agreed by the couples, Vivian and Moira will be legal parents to any tamaiti born from their reproductive relationship with Wilson and Johan, and Vivian will attempt to conceive using sperm donated by Johan. The Status of Children Act 1969 sets out rules for determining the legal status of parents in relation to their tamariki. However, where donated gametes have been used for conception, the deeming rules of the Status of Children Amendment Act 2004, Part 2, apply. These establish that a woman who conceives with donated gametes and bears a child, and her partner, on the proviso that she or he consented to the method used, are the child's legal parents (Gunn & Surtees, 2009; Surtees, 2011).

The deeming rules will also determine Johan's legal status as sperm donor. Despite the biogenetic relationship that he and Vivian will have with the tamaiti, his parenthood (unlike hers) will be extinguished under the Act.[2] He will have no rights, responsibilities or liabilities in respect of the child, and the child will lose those that would otherwise stem from him (Gunn & Surtees, 2009; Surtees, 2011). Significantly, this will occur irrespective of Johan, Wilson, Vivian and Moira's wish to be acknowledged jointly as parents and to co-parent together.

---

2 There are some exceptions to this rule, but they do not apply in this case.

Without legal parenthood, Johan and Wilson's rights as prospective fathers are largely reliant on the women upholding the agreed co-parenting intentions. Aware of their reliance on the women's goodwill, Wilson said, "We are vulnerable. There is an element of vulnerability, which is why again we think it is so important that we focus on the [adult] relationship[s]." To offset the challenge their vulnerability presents, the men will apply for guardianship of the child. Guardianship, while not bestowing full parental status, does provide legal authority over decision making and day-to-day care of a tamaiti, with some limits (Surtees, 2011).

The adults' plan to maintain separate households after the birth of a child reflects their current practice of cohabiting coupledom. This, in turn, troubles co-residence as a desirable standard for whānau. Retaining the adults' preferences for nuclear rather than communal living means the tamaiti will experience two homes, with a bedroom in each. As Wilson said, "I think both homes have to be homes for the child." The couples have, however, agreed that the child's primary base will be the women's home, an arrangement that many lesbians favour (Dempsey, 2010).

This family constellation's expected doing of family is clearly disruptive of the (hetero)norm in a range of ways, which is also the case for the second family constellation, whose members are already parenting a tamaiti.

Fern, Emma, Logan and Giles

The second family constellation included partners Fern and Emma, their 7-year-old son Giles, and two young adults he is related to. It also included Giles's father, Logan. Fern quipped that Logan, initially unknown to the women, "came lesbian recommended" through mutual friends. Giles's parents, like the members of the first family constellation, used the metaphor of dating to explain the early stages of their reproductive relationship—a relationship that, over time, has exceeded initial expectations. As Fern said, "it has panned out better than we planned or hoped for."

Fern, Emma and Logan also trouble the taken-for-granted primacy of heterosexual two-parent models. Their doing of family neither limits the number of parents to two nor limits the sharing of parenting to two. Like other parents in similar situations (Vaccaro, 2010), they find this approach mutually beneficial. Benefits extend to Giles, who said, "it's actually quite good having three parents, 'cause then that means you have more family members." As well as his three parents, Giles identified Logan's partner Bernard as "sort of" a parent. While Bernard agreed he had taken up a "parenting function" with Giles, he did not position himself as a fourth parent.

Neither these couples nor those in the first family constellation had legalised their couple relationships through a civil union, the only available mechanism to them in Aotearoa New Zealand. In troubling the taken-for-granted primacy of legal relationships between parents in their planning for or doing of family, both family constellations point to an existing adult bias in law. This bias—that a tamaiti should not have more than two parents, who are assumed to be in an intimate sexual relationship—fails to reflect particular situations of planned or actual multiple parenthood, where intimate sexual relationships exist alongside reproductive relationships. Such constraints, according to Hare and Skinner (2008), result from "adult-centric perspective[s] that discount children's reality" (p. 365).

This second family constellation, as with the first, highlights complex legal and biogenetic parent–child relationships, but with some key differences. Fern conceived Giles from sperm provided by Logan. As birth mother to Giles, she is his only legal parent and has a biogenetic relationship with him. Emma, Giles's non-birth mother, was unable to take up legal parenthood of him, as he was born before the Status of Children Amendment Act 2004, Part 2, which Moira (as previously outlined) expects to benefit from. Emma is, however, a guardian to Giles, as provided for under the Care of Children Act 2004. She has no biogenetic relationship with him. Logan is named in the women's wills as testamentary guardian to Giles, his only legal relationship with his biogenetic son. Giles's parents' relationships with him reflect the available options following his birth rather than their preferences. In a discussion about who should be included on their son's birth certificate, Logan voiced the parents' shared belief when he said, "I think it would be the best thing if you could name two mothers and a father."

Giles's parents' maintenance of separate households unsettles co-residence as a standard for families. Their doing of family sees Giles moving between households during the week, with more time spent in his mothers' home than in his father's. This arrangement is not dissimilar to the first family constellation's expected living arrangements. However, Giles has been advantaged by Logan's deliberate decision to live on the same street as Fern and Emma, thus enabling Giles to walk between his two homes. Giles described this as "quite cool".

> It's always nice to have a lot of houses 'cause you can go to different places and it's also nice having part of your family living in different places, 'cause that means you get to see some people sometimes and some more people another time, and then even more people another time.

He thought having one house "might get boring". Missing belongings were no problem. "If," he explained, "there's something really special at a particular house you want … you can go to their house and get it."

In their troubling of accepted benchmarks for whānau, the two family constellations discussed so far disrupt the (hetero)norm in similar ways. This is not the case for the last family constellation, whose approach to doing family differs markedly, thus illustrating the danger of assuming homogeneity among particular family forms.

Genevieve, Lynley, Pascal, Shamus and Henry

Civil union partners Genevieve and Lynley had long desired a family. Genevieve said, "My vision, when I met Lynley, was always that one day we would have a family ourselves." The birth of Henry, now a two-year-old, made the vision a reality.

Unlike the members of the first two family constellations, Genevieve and Lynley sought a reproductive relationship from among friends. Dempsey (2010) notes that this approach is "an oft-expressed first preference" (p. 1149). Also, unlike the first two family constellations, the women drove, rather than negotiated, the terms of the reproductive relationship subsequently established with their friends, partners Pascal and Shamus. Keen to make sure they would neither be fathers nor—as Genevieve said—"be a party to our parenting", she commented:

> *I spelt it out that, by giving us sperm, they were giving us sperm only. That in no way, shape or form could we ever offer them a title of father and they were never going to be parents. They would be ... seen as family friends, close family friends.*

Dempsey (2010) states:

> The formation of reproductive relationships will invariably give rise to some degree of reflexive engagement with the possibilities for chosen, created, negotiated, or intended relationships to children, yet these possibilities may ultimately be resolved with reference to quite normative considerations. (p. 1148)

This "solution" could be said to be the case for Genevieve and Lynley. In limiting the number of parents in the family constellation to their cohabiting legally recognised relationship, the women's doing of family reinforces the taken-for-granted primacy of two-parent models, legal relationships between parents and co-residence as "normal" standards. The following comments are illustrative:

I wanted to be sure in ourselves that Lynley and I had entered into a relationship that was recognised by [the] state ... we wanted to be sure ... that when we brought a child into the world, we'd done it correctly and properly and that our relationship was recognised. (Genevieve)

I guess we wanted, as the two parents, to bring a sense of normality as well—that we weren't three people bringing up a child, or two households bringing up a child. We wanted to stay very traditional with two parents, as traditional as you can be: two parents only. (Genevieve)

The women's reinforcement of "normal" standards is nevertheless disruptive given their lesbian relationship.

Genevieve and Lynley's legal parent–child relationships serve the women well. Unlike the options available to Fern, Emma, Logan and Giles, available options at the time of Henry's birth aligned with the women's plan to jointly share the central parenting relationship from within a single household. Lynley, as Henry's birth mother, is his legal parent and has a biogenetic relationship with him. Genevieve, named on Henry's birth certificate as second legal parent, as provided for by the Status of Children Amendment Act 2004, Part 2, has no biogenetic tie to Henry, thus disrupting the assumption that legal and biogenetic relationships go hand in hand.

Pascal and Shamus have no legal relationship with Henry. While both men acted as sperm donors to enable Henry's conception, only one has a biogenetic connection to him. His identity, in accordance with the women's wishes, has not been formally established. In this way, the women have deliberately undermined biogenetic ties as a relational base for parenthood.

While Pascal and Shamus accept their position in relation to Henry as part of the terms under which they donated sperm, it has brought some challenges. Pascal expected their status as "close family friends" would provide more contact with Henry than it has. Riggs (2008) found that disparities frequently existed between the contact expectations of lesbians and those of gay male donors, often despite agreements between all parties before the conception and birth of tamariki.

Across the three family constellations, an innovative reframing of forms of intimacy and care beyond the nuclear family model are to the fore. Despite evidence such as this, the ongoing privileging of this model in early childhood education through heteronormative discourses continues to exclude some whānau. The next section of this chapter considers how kaiako might respond to family diversity in ways that challenge exclusion.

Facilitating inclusive practice: "Kinship" as a resource for teachers

Facilitating inclusive practice in early childhood education settings requires kaiako to actively open up awareness of family diversity for all. As agents of change, teachers can—and should—adopt a tentative approach to thinking and talking about forms of doing family. This encourages others to engage in this way and enables a broadening of (discursive) spaces for this work. Teachers who are tentative in approach are better resourced to accept uncertainties—to be unsettled in mind and opinion—about the manifold possibilities for practising intimacy and care while setting aside judgements about these.

This situation creates opportunities for kaiako to recognise that many whānau are exploring unfamiliar terrain in their own practising of intimacy and care (Smart et al., 2001). Kaiako can not only join with these families to explore that terrain, regardless of their own experiences of it, but also resist "normative" standards for families and refuse to homogenise them. Such actions provide a key to disrupting heteronormative discourses and challenging exclusion. A tentative approach can also create opportunities for the development of sound relationships with whānau—relationships that truly allow families to be "seen", to be included and to belong.

Significantly, the family constellations at the heart of this chapter provide insight into the pitfalls of attempts to homogenise the emerging category of "lesbian- and gay-led families". These family constellations, although led by lesbians and gay men, are different. They are planning for, or engaging in, a range of different family practices. Some are very like the joint parenting of divorced or separated heterosexual couples, and some are much more like traditional nuclear families. Arguably, therefore, kaiako must think *beyond* particular family forms by assuming diversity in the families of *all* the tamariki who are accessing their programmes. In moving away from classification of groups of people based on law, biology, genetics and residency, a "kinship" framework may prove a useful resource.

Dempsey (2010) states that kinship "is more versatile than 'family' in attending to how people perceive themselves as connected to each other" (p. 1147). To work against heteronormative discourses and exclusion, teachers will need to focus on connections that matter to adults and tamariki regardless of whether those connections are conceptualised as "family" ties. This focus will mean paying careful attention to how adults and children are imagining, practising and expressing kin relationships. It will also mean developing awareness of the diversity of practices associated with the kin relationships in which adults and tamariki are embedded. Questions that kaiako could ask of key caregivers include:

- Who do you and your tamaiti claim as kin?
- How do you and your tamaiti name your kin?
- Who is in your child's network of care?
- What roles are taken up with your tamaiti?
- What should I know about those who live separately from your child's primary residence?

Focusing on connections that matter to adults and children will also require reviewing policies and administrative forms for evidence of normative assumptions about and homogenisation of families and the rewriting of these, as necessary. Finally, it will mean ensuring curriculum experiences (such as art, storytelling and drama) and materials and resources (such as posters, pictures, puzzles, books and the "family corner") represent diverse ways of being and doing family. Choosing to make visible the realities of adults' and children's connections with one another will respond to a legal and policy framework that upholds the rights of families to participate in inclusive early childhood education settings.

Conclusion

This chapter has documented some changing ways of planning for and doing family in contemporary Aotearoa New Zealand. Within a context of increasing family transformations, it is imperative that teachers recognise the shift away from the nuclear family model and the associated "normative" standards that these changes highlight. A focus on kinship can generate insights into the novel actions of family constellations that are practising relatedness, intimacy and care in ways that disrupt legal conventions and assumptions about biology and genetics. Early childhood kaiako can explore ways of thinking and talking about new forms of kinship that are expansive and generative—that open up rather than shut down possibilities for all families. Such an approach will both enhance inclusive practice and make ideas about innovative family relationships accessible to everyone—not just those who identify as lesbian or gay.

References

Agigian, A. (2004). *Baby steps: How lesbian alternative insemination is changing the world.* Middletown, CT: Wesleyan University Press.

Bogdan, R., & Biklen, S. (1998). *Qualitative research for education: An introduction to theory and methods* (3rd ed.). Needham Heights, MA: Allyn & Bacon.

Cohen, L., Manion, L., & Morrison, K. (2000). *Research methods in education* (5th ed.). New York, NY: RoutledgeFalmer.

Dempsey, D. (2005). *Beyond choice: Family and kinship in the Australian lesbian and gay "baby boom".* Unpublished doctoral thesis, La Trobe University, Melbourne, Victoria, Australia.

Dempsey, D. (2010). Conceiving and negotiating reproductive relationships: Lesbians and gay men forming families with children. *Sociology, 44*(6), 1145–1162.

Donovan, C. (2000). Who needs a father? Negotiating biological fatherhood in British lesbian families using self-insemination. *Sexualities, 3*(2), 149–164.

Edwards, J. (2000). *Born and bred: Idioms of kinship and new reproductive technologies in England.* Oxford, UK: Oxford University Press.

Edwards, J., Franklin, S., Hirsch, E., Price, F., & Strathern, M. (1999). *Technologies of procreation: Kinship in the age of assisted conception* (2nd ed.). London, UK: Routledge.

Fleming, R. (1999). *Families of a different kind: Life in the households of couples who have children from previous marriages or marriage-like relationships.* Waikanae: Families of the Remarriage Project.

Gunn, A. C., & Surtees, N. (2009). *"We're a family": How lesbians and gay men are creating and maintaining family in New Zealand.* Wellington: Kōmihana ā Whānau Families Commission.

Hare, J., & Skinner, D. (2008). "Whose child is this?" Determining legal status for lesbian parents who used assisted reproductive technologies. *Family Relations, 57,* 365–375.

Mason, J. (2008). Tangible affinities and the real life fascination of kinship. *Sociology, 42*(1), 29–45.

Mezey, N. J. (2008). *New choices, new families: How lesbians decide about motherhood.* Baltimore, MD: The Johns Hopkins University Press.

Ministry of Education. (1996a). Revised statement of desirable objectives and practices (DOPs) for chartered early childhood services in New Zealand. *Education Gazette, 139*(4), 3349–3550.

Ministry of Education. (1996b). *Te whāriki: He whāriki mātauranga mō ngā mokopuna o Aotearoa: Early childhood curriculum.* Wellington: Learning Media.

Ministry of Education. (1998). *Quality in action: Te mahi whai hua.* Wellington: Learning Media.

Morgan, D. H. J. (1996). *Family connections: An introduction to family studies.* Cambridge, UK: Polity Press.

Neuman, W. L. (1997). *Social research methods: Qualitative and quantitative approaches* (3rd ed.). Boston, MA: Allyn & Bacon.

Patton, M. Q. (2002). *Qualitative research and evaluation methods* (3rd ed.). Thousand Oaks, CA: Sage Publications.

Pollack, S., & Vaughn, V. (Eds.). (1987). *Politics of the heart: A lesbian parenting anthology*. Ithaca, NY: Firebrand Books.

Riggs, D. (2008). Using multinomial logistic regression analysis to develop a model of Australian gay and heterosexual sperm donors' motivations and beliefs. *International Journal of Emerging Technologies and Society, 6*(2), 106–123.

Ryan-Flood, R. (2005). Contested heteronormativities: Discourses of fatherhood among lesbian parents in Sweden and Ireland. *Sexualities, 8*(2), 189–204.

Silva, E. B., & Smart, C. (1999). The "new" practices and politics of family life. In E. B. Silva & C. Smart (Eds.), *The new family?* (pp. 1–12). London, UK: Sage Publications.

Smart, C. (2007). *Personal life: New directions in sociological thinking*. Cambridge, UK: Polity Press.

Smart, C., Neale, B., & Wade, A. (2001). *The changing experience of childhood: Families and divorce*. Cambridge, UK: Polity Press.

Stacey, J. (1990). *Brave new families: Stories of domestic upheaval in late twentieth century America*. New York, NY: Basic Books.

Strathern, M. (1992). *After nature: English kinship in the late twentieth century*. Cambridge, UK: Cambridge University Press.

Surtees, N. (2011). Family law in New Zealand: The benefits and costs for gay men, lesbians, and their children. *Journal of GLBT Family Studies, 7*(3), 245–263.

Surtees, N., & Gunn, A. C. (2010). (Re)marking heteronormativity: Resisting practices in early childhood education contexts. *Australasian Journal of Early Childhood, 35*(1), 42–47.

Vaccaro, A. (2010). Toward inclusivity in family narratives: Counter-stories from queer multi-parent families. *Journal of GLBT Family Studies, 6*(4), 425–446.

Weeks, J., Heaphy, B., & Donovan, C. (2001). *Same sex intimacies: Families of choice and other life experiments*. London, UK: Routledge.

Weston, K. (1991). *Families we choose: Lesbians, gays, kinship*. New York, NY: Columbia University Press.

Weston, K. (1993). Parenting in the age of AIDS. In A. Stein (Ed.), *Sisters, sexperts, queers: Beyond the lesbian nation* (pp. 156–186). London, UK: Penguin Books.

Wikler, D., & Wikler, K. (1991). Turkey baster babies. *The Millbank Quarterly, 69*(1), 5–40.

CHAPTER 4

Place-based education: Helping early childhood teachers give meaningful effect to the *tangata whenuatanga* competency of *Tātaiako* and the principles of *Te Whāriki*

Richard Manning

Introduction

In this chapter I draw on an experience I had as a father while visiting my son Jonathan's early childhood centre in Ōtautahi (Christchurch), Aotearoa New Zealand, during 2008. My visit followed a lesson in which my son was taught by another Pākehā father to perform "Ka Mate", the famous haka (posture dance) of the Ngāti Toa iwi. This lesson was problematic for the grandmother of one of my son's friends, affiliated to the Ngāti Kuri hapū of Ngāi Tahu.

My reflections in these pages are not designed to be critical of children performing "Ka Mate" or to be critical of early childhood teachers in general. Rather, they serve to explain why one centre's lack of knowledge about local Ngāi Tahu and Ngāti Toa tribal histories concerned both me and Jonathan's friend's grandmother. These reflections also serve to demonstrate why early childhood kaiako and leaders who display a similar lack of knowledge about the tangata whenua (people of the land) should be challenged by peers who are more familiar than they with the Ministry of Education's (2011) *Tātaiako: Cultural Competencies for Teachers of Māori Learners* and the principles underpinning *Te Whāriki* (Ministry of Education, 1996), this country's early childhood curriculum.

Although the Ministry of Education (2011) emphasises that the *Tātaiako* competencies "are not formal standards or criteria", they are "linked to the Graduating Teacher Standards and Registered Teacher Criteria developed by the New Zealand Teachers Council" (p. 4). Of most significance to this chapter is the Ministry's advice that the *tangata whenuatanga* competency is primarily about "affirming Māori learners as Māori … [and] providing [authentic] contexts for learning where the language, identity and culture of Māori learners and their whānau is affirmed" (p. 4). This objective is entirely consistent with the four principles underpinning *Te Whāriki* (Ministry of Education, 1996, pp. 40–43):

- *Whakamana (empowerment)*: "The early childhood curriculum empowers the child to learn and grow … Adults working with children should understand and be willing to … actively seek Māori contributions to decision making" (p. 40).

- *Kotahitanga (holistic development)*: "The early childhood curriculum reflects the holistic way children learn and grow … Adults working in early childhood education should have an understanding of Māori views on child development. … Activities, stories, and events that have connections with Māori children's lives are an essential and enriching part of the curriculum" (p. 41).

- *Whānau tangata (family and community)*: "The wider world of family and community is an integral part of the early childhood curriculum … Adults working with children should demonstrate an understanding of the different iwi and the meaning of whānau and whānaungatanga" (p. 42).

- *Ngā hononga (relationships)*: "Children learn through responsive and reciprocal relationships with people, places, and things ... The curriculum should include Māori people, places and artifacts and opportunities to learn and use the Māori language through social interaction" (p. 43).

To help kaiako give effect to these curriculum principles, the Ministry of Education (2011, p. 12) advises all "teachers" and "leaders" (including those in early childhood) to acquire and demonstrate historical knowledge of the places they work in and appropriately incorporate the knowledge of the local whānau, hapū and iwi they serve. The Ministry (2011, pp. 5, 12) suggests that place-based education (PBE) approaches may assist teachers and leaders meet the *tangata whenuatanga* competency.

However, most kaiako, irrespective of their sector, know little about the tenets of PBE. As Zucker (cited in Sobel, 2004, p. iii) explains, "[PBE] is distinguishable by the fact that it actively challenges conventional notions of education by requiring teachers and children to ask seemingly 'simple' questions like 'Where am I?' 'What is the nature of this place?' 'What sustains this community?'" Zucker adds that this process requires nothing less than a "re-storying process", whereby kaiako enable tamariki to "respond creatively to [the sometimes conflicting] stories of their home ground so that, in time, they are able to position themselves, imaginatively and actually within the continuum of nature and culture particular in that place" (p. iii). Tamariki and their teachers should become "part of the community", not "passive observers" of it.

Another facet of this chapter, then, is to help early childhood teachers and centre management to critically reflect on Zucker's questions and how these might relate to their efforts to respond constructively to the *tangata whenuatanga* competency guidelines and the principles of *Te Whāriki* (Ministry of Education, 1996). This assistance includes reference to some narratives of Ngāi Tahu and

Ngāti Toa researchers, easily obtained from the public domain, to illustrate the complex and sometimes conflicting views of different iwi narratives of past and place. The narratives also help illuminate the contemporary implications of the haka lesson mentioned earlier.

The kaiako responsible for this lesson were unaware of the whakapapa of this haka. They were also unaware of the whakapapa of Jonathan's friend and why "Ka Mate" was problematic for some members of that boy's whānau and hapū (Ngāti Kuri). The teachers were furthermore unaware of the historical sensitivities that members of the local Ngāi Tūāhuriri hapū can have about their tamariki being taught "Ka Mate".

Through acknowledgement of the struggles that Ngāti Toa have faced trying to protect the cultural integrity of "Ka Mate", this chapter also invites early childhood kaiako and centre management, locally and nationally, to consider why it is important to engage with whānau, hapū and iwi in curriculum design and delivery processes before implementing the Ministry of Education's (2011) new *Tātaiako* cultural competency guidelines, or enacting the curriculum principles of *Te Whāriki* (Ministry of Education, 1996), or both.

Why early childhood education teachers and centre management need to know about *tangata whenuatanga*

Imagine a photo of two four-year-old Pākehā boys hanging on the wall of a Christchurch early childhood education centre in 2008. The photo is surrounded by glossy cardboard sheets made resplendent with colourful kōwhaiwhai (painted scroll) patterns. A caption below the photo advises viewers that the boys are "wearing Māori costumes". These generic Māori costumes have obviously been made from felt material (non-traditional material) and were possibly put together in China.

The boys in the photo gesticulate with their arms and hands. Their faces are contorted as their eyes look upward. Their tongues protrude from their mouths. The caption below the photo also states, "Jonathan and William doing *the* haka" (my emphasis).

The caption implies that only one haka exists—the haka ("Ka Mate") that has long been performed by Aotearoa New Zealand's national rugby team, the All Blacks. The team performed this haka without the permission of Ngāti Toa until the signing of a memorandum of understanding between this iwi and the New Zealand Rugby Union on 17 March 2011 (Ngāti Toa Rangatira, 2011).

The boy in the photo named Jonathan is my youngest son. He and William were not performing *the* haka. Rather, they were role-playing a scene from *Badjelly the Witch*, a popular story for children written by the English comedian Spike Milligan (1995). My wife, Averill, was present when the photo was taken. She was surprised to see this photo later being singled out as evidence of "culturally responsive" practice just before a visit from Aotearoa New Zealand's Education Review Office, a government organisation which performs the role of an education setting inspectorate.

We should not have been surprised because we had only recently begun to see "Māori" content appearing in that centre. A week beforehand, a Pākehā father who played for a local rugby club had visited the centre to teach tamariki how to perform "Ka Mate". Although there were several tamariki Māori attending the centre, none of their parents or caregivers were consulted, a courtesy and consideration antithetical to the principles of *whakamana* and *whānau tangata* integral to *Te Whāriki* (Ministry of Education, 1996).

In my view, the centre's teachers and management should have consulted all parents and caregivers to identify a haka for their tamariki to learn. In so doing, they would have honoured not only the two principles just mentioned, but also those of *kotahitanga* and *ngā hononga*, likewise set out in the curriculum and outlined earlier in this chapter. The teachers I spoke to after the lesson appeared oblivious to the intent of the curriculum principles, especially those of *whakamana* and *whānau tangata*.

When the grandmother I spoke of at the beginning of this chapter told me, after the haka lesson, that she and her grandson were affiliated to the Ngāti Kuri hapū of Ngāi Tahu (based at Kaikōura), I was reminded that all haka, like people, have a whakapapa. "Ka Mate", Jonathan's friend's grandmother told me, was difficult for her because many of her tūpuna (ancestors) were decimated by a raiding party consisting of Ngāti Toa and its allies in 1828. The next section outlines some narratives associated with this event.

Ka mate! ('Tis death): The raid on Ngāti Kuri at Kaikōura (1828)

This raiding party, armed with muskets, was led by Te Rauparaha, who had earlier composed "Ka Mate" while fleeing some of his enemies at Lake Rotoaira in the central North Island (Collins, 2010, pp. 24–27; Grace, 1966, pp. 260–264). The raid on Ngāti Kuri occurred after their chief, Te Rerewaka, had threatened to rip Te Rauparaha's belly open with a shark's tooth should he arrive in Kaikōura to apprehend Te Rerewaka's relative, Te Kekerengū (Tau & Anderson, 2008, pp. 174–181; Te Rauparaha, 1980, pp. 34–36). Te Rauparaha's son, Tamihana Te Rauparaha, provided the following Ngāti Toa narrative of the attack on Ngāti Kuri residing at Kaikōura (Te Rauparaha, 1980, pp. 34–35):

> Te Rauparaha decided to go to Kaikōura. His war party consisted of 200 men travelling in five canoes. Te Pēhi [Te Rauparaha's uncle] also accompanied them … Thousands began to flee … *In this battle some 600 people fell, as well as a thousand women and children* [my emphasis].

"Ka Mate" is, therefore, a potent haka because it is still associated by some, but not all, Ngāi Tahu people with the suffering inflicted by Te Rauparaha and his allies during their raids into the Waitaha (Canterbury) region between 1828 and 1831. The grandmother of Jonathan's friend told me that for her, this choice of haka was culturally insensitive. She claimed that incidents such as this happen frequently in Christchurch because local Pākehā know so little about local Māori histories. She said that if the centre kaiako had asked her for advice, she would have shared her view.

This sharing would have been valuable, given the comments of a centre teacher about the lesson featuring "Ka Mate". She told me that she saw no harm in "all the children learning 'Ka Mate'" because it is widely viewed as a national icon, made famous by the All Blacks. I countered her argument by affirming the mana of "Ka Mate" while explaining that Ngāti Toa had undertaken legal action to protect the integrity of their haka from commercial exploitation and culturally offensive performances.

The teacher became defensive as I further explained why I considered that the centre's choice of haka had caused—and would likely cause more—anger among some whānau affiliated to the centre. Teaching this haka, although well intentioned, had risked "picking the scab off an old wound" inflicted during local historical conflict. The teacher responded that "the past is in the past" and the children had experienced a lot of "fun" learning the haka. Her stance, although conveyed indirectly, was dismissive of the principle in *Te Whāriki* of *whānau tangata*.

As a newcomer to Christchurch from the Wellington area, I quickly discovered that many other teachers in Canterbury (from all sectors of the education system) were misappropriating "Ka Mate". They were not consulting Ngāti Toa or engaging with local tribal authorities, such as Te Rūnanga o Ngāi Tūāhuriri (the tribal council of Ngāi Tūāhuriri, a prominent Ngāi Tahu hapū). As the newly appointed co-ordinator of the Treaty of Waitangi education programme at the University of Canterbury's College of Education, I found myself working alongside many Ngāi Tahu colleagues. Some also expressed concern at the misappropriation of "Ka Mate".

These colleagues, like the grandmother of Jonathan's friend, felt that using Māori cultural icons in this *ad hoc* manner was trampling on the mana of their iwi and of Ngāti Toa. This sort of behaviour, they believed, had the potential to needlessly reopen historical wounds. For example, when I spoke to my then Head of School about the haka incident at my son's early childhood centre, she said, with a hint of irony, "What a coincidence." She was in the middle of composing a polite, yet firm, email to the principal of a local secondary school. As the education spokesperson for her hapū, Ngāi Tūāhuriri, she was deeply concerned that the school was (like the early childhood centre) overlooking the sensitivities of some local whānau about local history.

The secondary school had signalled its intention to set a world record for the "world's largest haka" and intended to perform "Ka Mate" near the Kaiapoi Pā site—a major cultural landmark for all Ngāi Tahu people. However, emails from my Head of School and a group of concerned Māori parents persuaded the school to choose another haka. The school, to its credit, thus accepted that some local whānau and hapū members closely associate "Ka Mate" with the sacking of Kaiapoi Pā (an account of which follows), and that "Ka Mate" is therefore a provocative choice of haka and not conducive to *kotahitanga* (meaning unity, and which is a principle embedded within *Te Whāriki*). In so doing, the school demonstrated how to respond to the principle of *whakamana*, even though *whakamana* was not embedded in its curriculum.

Ka mate! The sacking of Kaiapoi Pā (1831)

Kaiapoi Pā was the first major settlement established by the Ngāi Tuhaitara ancestors of today's Ngāi Tūāhuriri hapū, following their migration from the lower North Island. The many tribal (and Pākehā) narratives of this event give conflicting reasons about why the pā was attacked. Given the limited length of this chapter, it suffices to state that, in 1828, after successfully attacking Kaikōura (described previously), Te Rauparaha and other related chiefs travelled south.

They presented themselves to the people of Kaiapoi Pā as friends, wishing to exchange pounamu (greenstone).

However, the Ngāi Tūāhuriri inhabitants of Kaiapoi Pā were well aware of the suffering these visitors had recently inflicted upon their Ngāti Kuri (fellow Ngāi Tahu) relatives at Kaikōura. They were also aware of the visitors' recent desecration of the nearby graveyard of a high-ranking Ngāi Tahu woman. This woman was the grandmother of Tamaiharanui, the senior chief residing at Kaiapoi (Collins, 2010, p. 83; Tau & Anderson, 2008, pp. 175–176). So those residing at Kaiapoi Pā suspected the visitors of treacherous intentions. The occupants of the pā devised a plan that included inviting the visiting chiefs to come inside it (Collins, 2010, pp. 83–84; Tau & Anderson, 2008, p. 176).

Te Pēhi, having previously befriended Tamaiharanui at Port Jackson (Sydney, Australia), felt safe to accept his friend's invitation to enter Kaiapoi Pā. He was accompanied by senior- and junior-ranking chiefs (Collins, 2010, p. 83). Te Pēhi and the other chiefs acted against the advice of Te Pēhi's nephew, Te Rauparaha. After experiencing a premonition, Te Rauparaha was wary of entering the pā. He advised Te Pēhi that he dreamt his hand had been bitten by a rat named "Pouhawaiiki" (Collins, 2010, pp. 84–85; Te Rauparaha, 1980, p. 35).

Accounts of the events that immediately preceded the violent death of Te Rauparaha's half-brother Te Aratangata, his cousin Te Pēhi and most other visiting chiefs inside the pā vary (Collins, 2010, pp. 83–85; Tau & Anderson, 2008, p. 176). However, there is a consensus that Te Pēhi and the others were killed and eaten according to the customary practices of that time (Collins, 2010, p. 84; Tau & Anderson, 2008, p. 180; Te Rauparaha, 1980, p. 35).

After mourning these deaths, and unsuccessfully attempting to force the inhabitants from the pā (with concentrated musket fire), Tamihana Te Rauparaha (1980, p. 36) noted that his father (Te Rauparaha) left the area, but only after issuing this warning to the inhabitants of Kaiapoi Pā: "Nourish your children for the time when I come back, because there will be no survivors. Those who have been murdered will be paid for by you and your female children." Te Rauparaha did return to the region in 1830, accompanied by a raiding party. They came on the brig *Elizabeth*, aided by the brig's opportunistic captain, John Stewart, and his crew. The so-called *Elizabeth* incident is well documented. It involved the abduction of Tamaiharanui and his wife and daughter after they had come aboard the *Elizabeth* at Akaroa, a settlement on Bank's Peninsula. The abduction was quickly followed by the killing and enslavement of many of the inhabitants of Tamaiharanui's kāinga at Takapūneke, nearby (Collins, 2010, pp. 87–90; Tau & Anderson, 2008, p.183). The three earlier-abducted family members died later, en route to Kāpiti Island or after arriving at that destination.

Collins (2010, p. 90) claims that despite the outcome of the *Elizabeth* incident, Te Rauparaha and his allies still desired to avenge the senior chiefs killed at Kaiapoi in 1828, especially after the desecration of Te Pēhi's bones "by Tūhawaiiki (of Ngāi Tuahuriri) and others in the Whakatū (Nelson) area". During the summer months of 1831 to 1832, two war parties consisting of warriors from different iwi travelled by sea and over land to besiege the previously impregnable pā at Kaiapoi.

According to Collins (2010, p. 93), the attacking force consisted of "100 of Te Rauparaha's Ngāti Toa from Kapiti, 200 Te Ātiawa, 100 Ngāti Raukawa and 100 Ngāti Toa from Taitapu." A siege, remembered for a flurry of attacks and counter-attacks, took place over a period of 3 months. Te Rauparaha eventually challenged his own warriors and allies to dig a series of saps (trenches) that zigzagged to the outer palisading of the Kaiapoi Pā. The saps, which were roofed for protection from sniper fire, allowed the attacking forces to pile dry wood against the wooden palisades, with the intent of eventually setting fire to them.

It was, however, the inhabitants of the pā who first decided to set fire to the piles of wood, hoping that the north-westerly winds would blow the flames away from the pā. But, as so often occurs in Waitaha, the wind changed direction, to a south-westerly, which blew the fire back onto the palisades. Much smoke and panic filled the pā. Collins (2010, p. 97) offers the following Ngāti Toa account of what happened next:

> The earth shook with the haka of 450 attacking warriors. Women and children seeking protection from their men hampered resistance. Some escaped through the swamp, only to be taken by the Rangitāne slaves of Ngāti Toa. Based on Stack's estimate of those living at Kaiapoi as about 1,000, the number of Ngāi Tahu killed was likely to have been between 300–350, with similar numbers captured and escaping.

Tau and Anderson (2008, pp. 185–186), writing from a Ngāi Tahu perspective, provide this conflicting account of the scale of the carnage that followed the fall of Kaiapoi Pā:

> Some of the thousand people who were then in the pā escaped by scaling the walls in the rear and making their way through the swamps; a few were taken prisoner, and about 600 were killed. Many of the prisoners were massacred on the little sand hill now occupied by a cow-shed, just opposite the junction of the road to the site of the pā [Preece's Road] and the main road [State Highway 1].

Irrespective of the debate surrounding the exact number of Ngāi Tahu people killed or enslaved, it is vital that *all* early childhood teachers and centre management know that events like this *did* occur in Waitaha and many other places around Aotearoa New Zealand, and not that long ago. A PBE approach may assist. A PBE approach would demand, for example, that the so-called "musket wars" (Ballara, 2003) of the past should *not* be treated by early childhood kaiako as "irrelevant" to curriculum implementation. This approach would instead require that such processes enact *Te Whāriki* (Ministry of Education, 1996) principles of *whakamana, kotahitanga, whānau tangata* and *ngā hononga*. The processes would also align with the *tangata whenuatanga* competency in *Tātaiako* (Ministry of Education, 2011). Ultimately, a PBE approach would demand nothing less than early childhood teachers becoming more familiar with local whānau and iwi narratives and being able to respond creatively to them. Such an approach would surely assist many early childhood kaiako and centre management to become part of their local Māori community, not just passive observers of it.

Ka ora! ('Tis life!): Using place-based education approaches to breathe life into the Treaty partnership

Lest we forget: Respecting local tribal histories of place

In similar spirit to the way that many Māori and non-Māori gather solemnly on Anzac Day to commemorate their ancestors and loved ones who died on foreign soils, early childhood teachers and centre management should be equally mindful and respectful of those thousands of New Zealanders (largely Māori) who died on local soil during the musket wars period (1806–1845). As Belich (1996, p. 157) has noted:

> The musket wars were the largest conflict ever fought on New Zealand soil. They killed more New Zealanders than World War One—perhaps about 20,000. They involved most tribes and caused substantial social and economic dislocation.

The Kaiapoi Pā site is a potent reminder of the southern campaigns of the musket wars. Just as Gallipoli is a solemn site for many New Zealanders, Kaiapoi Pā is a site that still holds memories for Ngāi Tahu people. Early childhood teachers around Aotearoa New Zealand need to appreciate that the musket wars, coupled with later wars against Crown forces, scarred the landscape and still inform territorial disputes.

Early childhood kaiako and centre management can easily obtain information about these wars by talking to local tribal custodians of knowledge, visiting libraries and cultural landmarks, searching for information on the internet and attending local hearings of the Waitangi Tribunal. Although Ngāi Tahu and Ngāti Toa gradually made a lasting peace in the 1840s, through strategic marriages and gift-making (Collins, 2010, p. 137; Tau & Anderson, 2008, p. 200), these iwi still contest each other's claims to lands in Te Waipounamu (the South Island). This state of affairs has been evident, for example, with regard to lands discussed in the Waitangi Tribunal's (2007) *Te Tau Ihu Customary Claims in the Statutory Ngāi Tahu Takiwā (Preliminary) Report.* I suspect that reading this sort of literature will help early childhood teachers and centre management gain a better understanding of why it is unwise to misappropriate Māori cultural icons, such as "Ka Mate", when haka composed and gifted by local whānau, hapū and iwi may respect local historical factors.

Ngāti Toa efforts to protect their haka and the Ngāi Tahu gift to the residents of Ōtautahi

Many New Zealanders have appropriately frowned on Hollywood movie moguls, United States universities, an Italian car company (Fiat) and the pop group the Spice Girls for their renditions of "Ka Mate". While these "foreign" misappropriations are rightly deemed "tacky", consideration should also be given to more localised misappropriations of "Ka Mate". Given the focus of this chapter, I propose that early childhood kaiako of Ōtautahi (and elsewhere) should consider embracing Māori icons in ways that are considered tika (just) by the tangata whenua of the area concerned, or other tribes with an interest in those icons, or both.

The New Zealand Rugby Union and a rugby club from my home town (Porirua) provide early childhood teachers and centre management with recent good examples of an approach that is tika and inherently place based. So, too, does the willingness of Ngāi Tahu to share their *tangata whenuatanga* in the wake of the series of major earthquakes in Canterbury in 2010 and 2011.

On 17 March 2011, the New Zealand Rugby Union and Ngāti Toa signed a memorandum of understanding to "protect" "Ka Mate". When announcing this event, Ngāti Toa stated:

> *Ka Mate* is an important part of New Zealand's cultural history. But above all of this, *Ka Mate* is a taonga of Ngāti Toa Rangatira and we as an iwi have an obligation to protect it. One of the iwi's long standing concerns is that *Ka Mate* has been used in a belittling and culturally offensive way. Fortunately the NZRU respects this position and has agreed to work with us to ensure that the integrity of *Ka Mate* is protected. (Ngāti Toa Rangatira, 2011)

In Porirua, Bidwell (2011) reported that:

> Norths' premier team coach Frank Rees said his boys had performed the haka 'four or five times' this season ... 'We're lucky enough that Ngāti Toa have given us the privilege of performing it and we've taken it in both hands,' Rees said. 'Ka Mate is owned by Ngāti Toa and we have a close relationship with them and there are a few boys from the iwi playing in our side. [Lock] Eldon Paea, who leads it, is from the pā [Takapūwāhia, Elsdon] and Ngāti Toa kaumatua Taku Parai is a longtime member of our club and used to play for us as well. He came and talked to us about it and we had a couple of workshops on it and we're just using it as a way to bind us more closely to our community.'

If the New Zealand Rugby Union and the Norths Rugby club can display respect for Ngāti Toa by *not* performing "Ka Mate" in ways that are culturally offensive, so too can early childhood teachers and centre management, nationwide. Likewise, it is worth recalling how, in the aftermath of the earthquake of 22 February 2011, Ngāi Tahu shared their haka "Tahu Pōtiki" with the people of Ōtautahi and New Zealand. This "super haka" helped raise the morale of and funds for people affected by the quakes. Sachdeva (2011) reported that:

> Hundreds of people have performed a haka in Christchurch as part of a nationwide event to support the city's quake-hit community. The super haka ... took place in Auckland, Wellington, Christchurch and

Dunedin at 12.30 pm today. Christchurch Mayor Bob Parker and Ngāi Tahu kaiwhakahaere (Chief Executive Officer) Mark Solomon lent their support to the Christchurch event, performing the haka with school pupils, businesses and residents. Parker said the 'sensational' haka was a strong show of support for the city's residents. 'It's hard to stay positive all the time, but this is the sort of energy we need.'

If a similar approach to the super haka were adopted by all Waitaha early childhood education centres, in partnership with their local Ngāi Tahu hapū, this would assist Ngāi Tahu efforts to revitalise their *tangata whenuatanga*. Early childhood kaiako and centre management must recognise that if they misappropriate Māori cultural icons, they will not be meeting the indicators of the *tangata whenuatanga* competency set by the Ministry of Education (2011). Nor will they be adhering to the principles central to *Te Whāriki* (Ministry of Education, 1996). This lack, in turn, would subvert the intent of the Crown's principles of partnership, active protection and participation embedded within the principles for Crown action on the Treaty of Waitangi (Hayward, 2009).

Given that so many official guidelines specify that early childhood teachers and centre management *are* required to "protect" Māori culture, the following whakataukī provides a pertinent close to this chapter. As Mead and Grove (2001, p. 39) propose, this whakataukī suggests that "those who are content with mediocre returns need not be attentive to their work, but those who strive for more desirable goals must ever be alert for possibilities". It goes:

E moe te mata hī aua, e ara te mata hī tuna.

The mullet-fisher sleeps but the eel catcher is alert.

Acknowledgements

I would like to acknowledge the following people, who were consulted during the writing of this chapter: Rikiihia Tau (Ngāi Tūāhuriri: kaumātua (elder)), Taku Parai (Ngāti Toa: kaumātua); Te

Waari Carkeek (Ngāti Raukawa: tumuaki (manager), Te Rūnanga o Ngāti Raukawa, Ōtaki); Dr Te Maire Tau (Ngāi Tūāhuriri: Director of the Ngāi Tahu Research Centre, University of Canterbury); Lynne-Harata Te Aika (Ngāi Tūāhuriri: Head of School, Aotahi, School of Māori and Indigenous Studies, University of Canterbury); and Professor Angus Macfarlane (Te Arawa: Professor of Māori Research, University of Canterbury).

References

Ballara, A. (2003). *Taua: Musket wars, "land wars" or "tikanga"?* Auckland: Penguin Books.

Belich, J. (1996). *Making peoples: A history of the New Zealanders from Polynesian settlement to the end of the nineteenth century.* Auckland: Allen Lane/ The Penguin Press.

Bidwell, H. (2011, 13 June). Norths challenge opponents with *Ka Mate* haka. *Dominion Post.* Retrieved from http://www.stuff.co.nz/sport/rugby/ news/5134237/Norths-challenge-opponents-with-Ka-Mate-haka

Collins, H. (2010). *Ka mate ka ora!: The spirit of Te Rauparaha.* Wellington: Steele Roberts.

Grace, T. H. (1966). *Tūwharetoa: A history of the Māori people of the Taupo district.* Wellington: A. H. & A. W. Reed.

Hayward, J. (2009). *The principles of the Treaty of Waitangi (appendix).* Retrieved from http://www.waitangi-tribunal.govt.nz/doclibrary/public/ Appendix(99).pdf

Mead, H. M., & Grove, N. (2001). *Ngā pēpeha a ngā tīpuna: The sayings of the ancestors.* Wellington: Victoria University Press.

Milligan, S. (1995). *Badjelly the witch.* Auckland: Penguin Books New Zealand.

Ministry of Education. (1996). *Te whāriki: He whāriki mātauranga mō ngā mokopuna o Aotearoa: Early childhood curriculum.* Wellington: Learning Media.

Ministry of Education. (2011). *Tātaiako: Cultural competencies for teachers of Māori learners.* Wellington: Ministry of Education.

Ngāti Toa Rangatira. (2011). *Ngāti Toa and the New Zealand Rugby Union enter new era of relationship with Ka Mate.* Retrieved from http://www.ngatitoa.iwi. nz/ngati-toa-and-new-zealand-rugby-union-enter-new-era-of-relationship-with-ka-mate/

Sachdeva, S. (2011, 19 May). Hundreds do super haka: Four centres in joint haka. *Press*. Retrieved from http://www.stuff.co.nz/the press/news/5026314/Hundreds-do-super-haka

Sobel, D. (2004). *Place based education: Connecting classrooms and communities*. Great Barrington, MA: The Orion Society.

Tau, T. M., & Anderson, A. (2008). *Ngāi Tahu: A migration story: The Carrington text*. Wellington: Bridget Williams Books.

Te Rauparaha, T. (1980, P. Butler, Ed.). *Life and times of Te Rauparaha: By his son Tamihana Te Rauparaha*. Wairua, Martinborough: Alister Taylor.

Waitangi Tribunal. (2007). *Te tau ihu o te waka a Maui: Te tau ihu customary claims in the statutory Ngāi Tahu Takiwa*. Wellington: Legislation Direct.

CHAPTER 5

Huakina mai: Opening doorways for children's participation within early childhood settings—economic disadvantage as a barrier to citizenship

Glynne Mackey and Colleen Lockie

Introduction

A recent report by the Child Poverty Action Group (Dale, O'Brien, & St John, 2011) makes clear that Aotearoa New Zealand's record of caring for its young citizens is far from exemplary. The report presents data that position Aotearoa New Zealand at 28th place (out of the 30 OECD countries listed) for child wellbeing outcomes. As the report's authors elaborate, many tamariki in this country live lives marked by poverty. These children, they continue, tend to be disadvantaged because of family circumstances of unemployment, high-cost and low-standard housing, low household incomes and poor health care. The authors devote a complete chapter to the role of early childhood education. They argue that Aotearoa New Zealand, as a nation, needs to be "doing more" in the early childhood years, commonly accepted as a vital period for establishing children's long-term wellbeing.

This report is just one of a growing number that present a less than favourable picture of Aotearoa New Zealand's present provision in health, welfare and education. Examples of other reports are the Salvation Army's *Monopoly Games in the Nursery* (Walden, 2011), the annual *Children's Social Health Monitor* (New Zealand Child & Youth Epidemiology Service, 2011), and the Office for the Commissioner for Children's report on children and young people's experience of poverty (Egan-Bitran, 2010). These reports highlight the barriers within social and education policy that tend to create cumulative disadvantage for tamariki from economically disadvantaged backgrounds. Walden (2011), for example, has this to say:

> New Zealand children who are members of low socio-economic households or who live in low socio-economic communities are accessing early childhood education … less than other New Zealand children. The consequence of this results in children being less successful in their early years of school and opens the door to lifelong educational and economic disadvantage. (p. iv)

This comment and similar ones in the other reports cited above support an argument developed by James and Prout (1997). They contend that tamariki and whānau who are restricted from fully participating in educational and care settings, including early childhood ones, are simultaneously prevented from practising within those settings—and in society itself—the rights and responsibilities that are an expression of citizenship. For Kjørholt (2005), the status of citizenship gives individuals, no matter what their age, the power to be themselves—autonomous subjects with a voice in decision making. When, Kjørholt says, young children are not viewed as citizens, they are denied a voice in making the decisions that affect them. We consider this a problem for practising inclusion.

Nutbrown and Clough (2009) argue, and we agree, that even very young children can express their ideas and contribute to decision making. They maintain that early childhood education and care settings (hereafter referred to as early childhood settings) provide opportunities for our youngest citizens to engage with democratic processes. These processes, the authors explain, are those that enable participants to share knowledge, understand and accept other perspectives, and voice opinions. They take place within inclusive communities that listen, care and act for the collective good.

Here we focus on tamariki and their whānau who, because of economic disadvantage, are often limited in terms of opportunity and ability to draw on the resources and processes that enable them to attend and actively participate in early childhood settings of their choice. We explore notions of childhood and discuss how people's views on childhood can adversely or positively mediate that participation.

Much of the discussion in this chapter is premised on the idea that the participation of children in early childhood settings occurs on two levels (see, in this regard, Thomas, 2007). The first is engagement with the curriculum; the second is involvement in the making of decisions about issues that affect their early childhood setting. This chapter is also written from the perspective of *equity pedagogy* (Hyland, 2010), an approach to teaching that assumes that injustice is endemic and systemic, functioning to privilege some groups and marginalise others. From an equity pedagogy perspective, if teachers and educational settings do not consciously strive to counter injustice, then they, by default, support it. Equity pedagogy, in short, means taking action to limit inequalities.

Impacts of economic disadvantage on active participation

Poverty affects access to resources and services. Access to resources and services affects participation in a range of experiences, including sport, recreation, education and health. Transience, poor health and limited ability to join (for example) organised sport and recreation (for household members of any age) provide barriers to those experiences that encapsulate citizenship in action, and the ability to practise citizenship in a supported context (Ridge, 2006).

In Aotearoa New Zealand, the available data suggest that more and more tamariki are experiencing these barriers. The number of children classified as living in conditions of poverty has steadily increased in this country in recent years. Since 2009 the estimated annual rate of increase has encompassed 1 to 2 percent of all tamariki living in Aotearoa New Zealand. This percentage translates into an additional 10,000 to 20,000 children each year. Today, the number of children experiencing poverty in this country is estimated to be 200,000, or 25 percent of all children residing in this country (Dale et al., 2011; Johnson, 2011a; OECD, 2011; Walden, 2011).

The most significant impacts of poverty typically fall on households where no one is in paid employment, or where there has been long-term reliance on government benefits, or both (Krishnan, Jensen, & Rochford, 2002; O'Brien & Salonen, 2011). These impacts are affecting an increasing number of children in households with little disposable income. Various researchers argue that this situation is associated with increases in the cost of life's necessities, including food and housing (whether for mortgage or rent). The impact of these increases is heightened by the country's overall low-wage economy (Egan-Bitran, 2010; Fletcher & Dwyer, 2008; Johnson, 2011b).

Another trend of concern for Aotearoa New Zealand is its rate of income inequality (i.e., the gap between the "haves" and "have nots"). Today, Aotearoa New Zealand has the fourth highest rate of income inequality in the OECD (Wilkinson & Pickett, 2010), with the strongest rate of acceleration in this country occurring from the mid-1980s (OECD, 2011, p. 66). Wilkinson and Pickett's analysis of their data provide convincing support for their claim that the greater the inequity *between* income groups in any given country, the greater the negative effects on all measures of health, education, violence, child mortality, teenage pregnancy, drug use, imprisonment, crime, social mobility and mental health. And these effects are experienced, to varying degrees, by *all the citizens* of that country, not just the poor.

The rate at which income inequality in Aotearoa New Zealand is growing suggests that children today are experiencing the effects of inequity in ways that their parents never did. Equally concerning are the apparent cumulative effects of disadvantage over time and through the generations. Also, the younger the child, the more negative the effect that poverty is likely to have on a wide range of measures, particularly health, stable housing, physical safety and education.

Reports arising out of the Christchurch Health and Development Study support these claims. Since mid-1977 the study's research team has been following a cohort of 1,000 people born in Canterbury hospitals at that time. A data analysis conducted during the year when the participants reached 21 years of age (Maloney, 2004) explored the impact of family income in childhood on outcomes for these young people. Disadvantage was observable and measurable across indices of welfare, health and education. Another Aotearoa New Zealand research study supports these findings of multiple disadvantage. Krishnan et al. (2002) show from their analyses of available data that the children who are most disadvantaged are those from families whose experience of low income and government benefits is long term.

Reference to the Matthew Effect is a useful means of exploring the discussion related to the cumulative disadvantage of inequality. The Matthew Effect refers to a biblical text (Matthew 25:29) which claims that everyone who has shall have in abundance, whereas those who have not shall have taken away that which they have. This effect has been used to describe the cumulative nature of advantage and disadvantage—as noted earlier, self-perpetuating cycles of growing advantage and disadvantage produce widening inequalities over time and generations (Rigney, 2010; Walden, 2011). The effect has also received attention from Thrupp (2007, 2008) with respect to Aotearoa New Zealand's education system.

When writing on the issue of economic disadvantage, we have reflected on how the Matthew Effect affects our youngest citizens. We acknowledge that this effect is not simply about money, but also about the multiplicity of available knowledge, wisdom and wealth at the community level. The sharing of such resources, in our view, supports the ability to practise citizenship. This is because the active intergenerational transfer of knowledge, wisdom and wealth within communities can alleviate some cumulative disadvantage stemming from limited resources at the family level. Such transfer occurs in settings where people from a wide range of ages share time together. It concerns us, therefore, that children who spend long hours in early childhood settings may have less time to spend in intergenerational transfer situations.

This point is an important one with respect to the cumulative nature of disadvantage and its implications for early childhood settings—implications that are complex and the discussion of which is limited in this chapter. However, equity pedagogy suggests that early childhood kaiako have responsibility for taking steps to lessen the Matthew Effect. This is because, as we describe and discuss in the next sections of this chapter, kaiako can intentionally provide programmes that go some way towards removing barriers to participation. Fletcher and Dwyer (2008) capture our thinking in their aspiration for early childhood settings: "High quality early childhood and education services can be a powerful equaliser, reducing disadvantages among children in low income families" (p. 66).

The concern at this point, of course, is ascertaining how early childhood teachers can realise what many might consider to be a daunting aim. We think that one of the most important first steps in this direction is for kaiako to critically reflect on their views of "childhood". How agentic do they think children can and should be with respect to actively participating in the everyday contexts in which they live and learn?

Notions of childhood and children's right to participate

According to Alderson (2005), traditional Western notions of childhood position children as vulnerable, immature, incompetent, ignorant and without rational thought—of not yet having attained the status of an adult. Adult status is usually assigned to those who, having gone through rites of passage that mark transition from childhood, through adolescence and on to adulthood, can (supposedly) make a worthwhile contribution as "fully fledged" citizens. Dale et al. (2011, p. 6) express similar ideas:

> Children appear in the policy discussion in complex ways: as burdens on their parents, as adults-to-be; as victims of adult choices about relationships; and as threats to social order and stability. Children do not often appear simply as children with their own voices, their own agency, and their right to a happy, safe childhood.

Alderson (2005) claims that adults in many societies worldwide continue to hold fast to constructs of childhood that allow adults to claim power in adult–child relationships. The constructs make for "underestimated and over controlled" children (p. 131). Glynne, writing elsewhere (Mackey, 2011), concurs. Children's potential, she says, is restricted if their participation in education is bounded by adult perceptions and expectations of what children can/cannot and should/should not do at certain ages and stages.

Smith (2007) goes further when she argues that this power dynamic works against the articles of the United Nations Convention of the Rights of the Child (UNCRC), promulgated in 1989 and to which Aotearoa New Zealand is a signatory. Her reason for this claim is that the power dynamic undermines the rights of our youngest citizens to have their voices heard on the matters that directly concern them.

Smith calls on early childhood professionals to ensure the principles of UNCRC inform their practice. She sees the convention as a powerful tool for change in early childhood policy and practice.

The most recent (February 2011) United Nations report to Aotearoa New Zealand on meeting its responsibilities under UNCRC echoes Smith's messages:

> *The Committee notes with regret that the views of children are not adequately respected within the family, in schools and in the community. The Committee also regrets there is no means by which children can express their views in the public domain*, that the State party does not systematically take into consideration children's views when formulating laws and policies that affect them and that their right to be heard in judicial and administrative proceedings is not sufficiently respected.
>
> The Committee recommends that the State party, in accordance with Article 12 of the Convention … [and] its general comment No. 12 (2009) on the right of the child to be heard:
>
> (a) Promote, facilitate and implement, in legislation as well as in practice, within the *family, schools, and the community as well as in institutions and in administrative and judicial proceedings, the principle of respect for the views of the child*; and
>
> (b) Systematically consider the views of the child in formulating laws and policies.
>
> (UNCRC, 2011, pp. 5–6, emphasis ours)

James and Prout (1997) bring clarity to considerations of how children's voices can be given prominence in their discussion of children as "becoming" and children as "being". They, like Alderson (2005), argue that in Western culture tamariki generally are seen as *becoming* an adult, as *becoming* more competent. This perspective, they explain, influences how we relate to infants, toddlers and young children. Within early childhood settings, this viewpoint can manifest itself in policy and practice in ways that do not value this period of children's lives as one critical for their learning and for their social development and participation.

According to James and Prout (1997), children are not passive recipients of social norms, but are actively engaged in creating their own identities and those of others. Their identities are linked to their engagement with everyday experiences within their culture and within their setting (see also, in this regard, Smith, 2007). Tamariki do not see themselves as becoming; instead, they strongly situate their identities in the act of *being*.

When adults (kaiako, whānau) view children as *being* rather than *becoming* and as *beings* in their own right (James & Prout, 1997; Lansdown, 2004; Smith, 2007), they tend to engage in discourses that focus on children as having agency, of being competent. They are also more likely to position themselves as sharing power and decision making with children. Lansdown (2004) argues that children who have the opportunity to express their needs and desires—to have a "voice"—are better able to take care of themselves and are less vulnerable to abuse. Lansdown also observes that if children cannot participate in social settings, such as caregiving, preschool and school, they are denied the opportunity to *actively* practise the skills required for being citizens who are involved in democratic processes.

In Aotearoa New Zealand, having tamariki and their whānau actively participate in daily decision making is a strong principle underpinning *Te Whāriki*, this country's early childhood curriculum (Ministry of Education, 1996). Active participation in daily decision making is an inclusive process because decisions take account of local, cultural and time-bound factors. The outcome is a flexible, fluid approach to curriculum, programme, management and governance, an approach that *Te Whāriki* refers to as the individually woven mat on which each early childhood setting stands. Active participation also assumes intimate connections and interdependent relationships between tamariki, whānau and community. These are represented in *Te Whāriki* in terms of Urie Bronfenbrenner's ecological model of human development (Bronfenbrenner, 1979).

One thing that active participation is *not* is enrolment or attendance. The distinction is an important one because enrolment numbers in early childhood settings are often presented as participation. However, enrolment does not equate with attendance, attendance does not equate with participation, and participation does not equate with active participation. Table 1 illustrates these differences.

Kaiako who understand these distinctions are likely also to engage in participation for citizenship discourses that acknowledge that children have agency. This knowledge allows teachers to understand children as competent to make a contribution as active members of society (James & Prout, 1997). Understanding this competence gives powerful guidance in adult–child relationships and practices within educational settings, including early childhood ones. In the next section, we draw on ideas and commentary from several sources to show how early childhood programmes can be modified so that tamariki, including very young ones, can practise and exhibit competence.

Ideas on developing equity pedagogy in Aotearoa New Zealand

In her discussion of *Te Whāriki* as a "technology of citizenship" or as a "democratic tool", Duhn (2006) reminds us that the early childhood curriculum itself provides much that is useful in guiding the development of such programmes and, from there, supporting children to participate in those settings and in their local communities in meaningful ways.

Guidance also comes from current empirical and qualitative data on economic disadvantage. The available information is constantly updated as governments come and go and as statistical data are published and analysed. Discerning teachers therefore need to read widely to fully understand the complex nature of children

Table 1: Levels of participation in early childhood education

Enrolment	Attendance	Participation (ecological)	Active participation (ecological, equitable, pedagogic and inclusive)
Tamariki are enrolled at an early childhood education setting.	Tamariki regularly attend an early childhood education setting.	Tamariki and their whānau engage in a range of experiences *offered* by the early childhood education setting.	Tamariki and their whānau actively engage in decision making related to daily matters, curriculum/ programme, and management and governance. They *are thus able to make a difference to the experiences that are offered* within the early childhood education setting, and thereby practise citizenship.

in economically disadvantaged situations. They need to access recent government documents, reports from non-governmental organisations, and academic research conducted within the Aotearoa New Zealand context.

Early childhood settings are, we believe, well situated to take a leading role in working with communities to identify and remediate inequity. In our experience as early childhood kaiako and teacher-educators, early childhood settings tend to have close and frequent contact with parents, caregivers and other whānau in the community. Potentially they have a more holistic appreciation of equity for families within that community. Our claim receives support from commentary in Walden (2011), who criticises the propensity to take a one-size-fits-all approach to educational policy. She states that such an approach is rarely effective because it does not take into account inequities operating at the level of family and community. Walden also recommends that the "Government needs to change from an emphasis on education as a commercial commodity to emphasising citizens' rights for equitable provision" (p. v).

Drawing on discourses of children's rights and active citizenship as they relate to child poverty, O'Brien and Salonen (2011) also argue that policy makers, practitioners, social welfare agencies and kaiako need to explore these aspects further to better understand their implications for poverty and children's long-term wellbeing. Their case study of the influence of targeted and means-tested welfare policies and practices on families in Aotearoa New Zealand and Sweden leads them to conclude that these tend to disengage the adults in those families from active citizenship. That disengagement, in turn, deprives the children in those families of role models of active citizenship in their daily lives. The implication of O'Brien and Salonen's findings for early childhood programmes is the need for those developing and delivering them to provide opportunities for all tamariki to see and to practise models of active citizenship in meaningful contexts within early childhood settings and their local community.

Gordon's research (2004) highlights the aspirations of a small group of socioeconomically vulnerable mothers who aspired to a different and potentially better life for their children than the one they had experienced. Gordon notes the importance of support and intervention at an early age to ensure achievement and wellbeing. The role of early childhood settings, she concludes, should be to support the achievement of this aspiration, by working in collaborative partnerships with these parents who have "hope and low family resources" (p. 62).

As early childhood kaiako, how might we support these aspirations and what might that support look like from day to day within an equity pedagogy curriculum? The following six suggestions may provide some insight into useful practices.

1. *Restorative justice:* Ritchie, Lockie and Rau (2011) present an argument for bringing into early childhood settings "a peace in education" curriculum, based on an ethic of care. Aspects of peace in education tend to be evident in settings that use the principles of restorative practice/justice to manage conflicts on a daily basis. Restorative justice supports the voices of all to be heard respectfully, so that solutions can be collaboratively constructed, providing opportunities for citizenship in action. In this regard the framework developed by Restorative Schools (2011) is useful. It requires all individuals involved to respond to these questions:
   - What happened? (Tell the story.)
   - Who do we think has been affected? (Explore the harm.)
   - What do we need to do to put things right? (Repair the harm.)
   - How can we make sure this doesn't happen again? (Move forward.)

2. *Interconnectedness of living things:* Growing edible gardens in early childhood settings is a simple but effective way to illustrate the interconnectedness of living things (both human and vegetable). Collaboratively planning what is to be planted, monitoring water and nutrient needs, creating mulch from compost, keeping data about the productivity of particular vegetables and fruits, and making plans for cooking, preserving or sharing the harvest provide opportunities for tamariki to experience, at a local level, global food issues. These include overabundance, scarcity, collective labour for a common goal and the systems thinking necessary for equitable food production and distribution.

3. *Children as critical consumers:* Early childhood settings have budgets to purchase a wide range of resources for the curriculum. Looking through resource catalogues, investigating the use and condition of existing resources and deciding on budget priorities all provide opportunities for children to have their voices heard and to make collective decisions. If indoor and outdoor environments are to be redesigned, children can be appropriately involved in planning and purchasing decisions.

4. *Affordable technologies:* Sophisticated but inexpensive weather stations are available for tamariki and kaiako to use. These monitor for example precipitation, temperature, wind, sunshine and the level of ultraviolet radiation. When tamariki are supported to collect weather data every day, they have the opportunity to be actively involved in planning daily programmes, monitoring the need for sunblock and hats, and graphing data to inform future events.

5. *Engagement with local issues:* News is available in an increasing variety of forms—newspapers, web-based, and social media. Newspapers, however, provide a concrete, ongoing, ever-changing and locally relevant access point for young tamariki to become aware of issues and to express opinions. The 2010/11 earthquakes in Canterbury provide an example. Newspapers have not only let tamariki give voice to their experiences of and thoughts on these events, but have also provided impetus for children to be involved in public consultation on the rebuilding of Christchurch city. Early childhood settings in the city have used features in local papers on rebuild ideas to help them encourage and support children to make submissions on these plans.

6. *International conventions:* Some books for tamariki present the complex text of international conventions in understandable forms. These books are readily available for the United Nations Convention on the Rights of the Child, the Human Rights

Declaration, and the Earth Charter. Early childhood settings that actively plan to support children to read and understand these international declarations, and to apply their understanding in daily practice, provide opportunities for the youngest of tamariki to develop the sense of a *being* (rather than a *becoming*) citizen, because these texts are developed particularly for that purpose.

Finally, we claim that early childhood settings able to implement programmes that support active citizenship in ways similar to the above examples are those that are adequately funded and therefore able to employ qualified and experienced teachers. We consider that directly targeting vulnerable tamariki and their whānau comes at the expense of sufficient funding for early childhood settings. For a range of complex reasons that cannot be explored in this chapter, early childhood settings are among the sites best placed to offer the type of rich and complex programmes that ameliorate some cumulative barriers to participation created by economic disadvantage.

Conclusion

As various commentators and researchers remind us, there are many reasons why active participation as citizens by young children is a morally, ethically and financially sound course of action for any country. When Aotearoa New Zealand signed the United Nations Convention of the Rights of the Child, it made a commitment to develop policies that support children as active participants and citizens in society. As such, there needs to be greater active recognition and amelioration of family circumstances of impoverishment that disadvantage young children. When children, because of impoverishment, are excluded from accessing resources that enable them to participate as social and contributing "beings" within their communities, they are excluded from practising the skills of citizenship and, in the longer term, from participation in democratic citizenship. This form of citizenship encompasses respectful, responsive and reciprocal relationships with others, supports agency and competence, and invites active participation and inclusion.

Kaiako and other people in early childhood settings need to recognise how difficult it can be for vulnerable families to provide models of active citizenship for their tamariki. They then need to recognise the valuable role they can play in providing opportunities for tamariki to witness and practise the behaviours that constitute active citizenship. Role modelling participative citizenship and strengthening collaborative partnerships with families are also important components of what early childhood settings can do to lower the barriers that prevent vulnerable families and children from engaging as active citizens in their homes and communities.

We caution, however, that quality early childhood education programmes of the kind just described can never be a panacea for disadvantage and disengagement. Such programmes alone cannot fully overcome the barriers to participation (in the deepest sense of citizenship) experienced by many children growing up in financially impoverished contexts. These barriers are formed from the difficulties associated with, for example, parenting alone, finding work (even part time), trying to survive on the minimum wage, and endeavouring to access what help is available from welfare and other support agencies. But when early childhood kaiako acknowledge that what they do *now* is important—because tamariki, even very young ones, are human *beings*, not human *becomings*, and when they, from there, practise equity pedagogy—they help disrupt the circuit of intergenerational poverty and alienation. In this way, they contribute to ensuring not only a positive present but also (possible) positive futures for our youngest children, regardless of the personal wealth of their whānau.

References

Alderson, P. (2005). Children's rights: A new approach to studying childhood. In H. Penn (Ed.), *Understanding early childhood: Issues and controversies* (pp. 127–141). Oxford, UK: Oxford University Press.

Bronfenbrenner, U. (1979). *The ecology of human development: Experiment by nature and design.* Cambridge, MA: Harvard University Press.

Dale, C. M., O'Brien, M., & St John, S. (Eds.). (2011). *Left further behind: How policies fail the poorest children in New Zealand.* Auckland: Child Poverty Action Group.

Duhn, I. (2006). The making of global citizens: Traces of cosmopolitanism in the New Zealand early childhood curriculum, *Te Whāriki. Contemporary Issues in Early Childhood, 7*(3), 191–202.

Egan-Bitran, M. (2010). *This is how I see it: Children, young people and young adults' views and experiences of poverty.* Wellington: Office of the Commissioner for Children.

Fletcher, M., & Dwyer, M. (2008). *A fair go for all children: Actions to address child poverty in New Zealand.* Wellington: Office of the Commissioner for Children and Barnados New Zealand.

Gordon, L. (2004). Why did Kath, Mary and Kim get so little education (and is there hope for their children)? *New Zealand Journal of Teachers' Work, 1*(1), 52–63.

Hyland, N. (2010). Social justice in early childhood classrooms: What the research tells us. *Young Children, 65*(1), 82–90.

James, A., & Prout, A. (1997). *Constructing and reconstructing childhood: Contemporary issues in the sociological study of childhood* (2nd ed.). London, UK: Falmer Press.

Johnson, A. (2011a). *Stalled: A state of the nation report from the Salvation Army.* Wellington: The Salvation Army Social Policy and Parliamentary Unit.

Johnson, A. (2011b, November). *The cost of everything and the value of nothing: How little economics can tell us about the value of early childhood education.* Paper presented to the Early Childhood Education Federation, Wellington.

Kjørholt, A. (2005). The competent child and "the right to be oneself": Reflections on children as fellow citizens in an early childhood centre. In A. Kjørholt, P. Moss, & A. Clark (Eds.), *Beyond listening: Children's perspectives on early childhood services.* Bristol, UK: The Policy Press.

Krishnan, V., Jensen, J., & Rochford, M. (2002). Children in poor families: Does the source of family income change the picture? *Social Policy Journal of New Zealand, 18*, 118–147.

Lansdown, G. (2004). Participation and young children. *Early Childhood Matters*, 103, 4–14.

Mackey, G. (2011). To know, to decide, to act: The young child's right to participate in action for the environment. *Environmental Education Research*, 13(4), 529–544.

Maloney, T. (2004). Are the outcomes of young adults linked to the family income experienced in childhood? *Social Policy Journal of New Zealand*, 22, 55–82.

Ministry of Education. (1996). *Te whāriki: He whāriki mātauranga mō ngā mokopuna o Aotearoa: Early childhood curriculum.* Wellington: Learning Media.

New Zealand Child & Youth Epidemiology Service. (2011). *The Children's Social Health Monitor: 2011 update.* Dunedin: Author. Retrieved from http://www.nzchildren.co.nz/userfiles/ Childrens%20Social%20Health%20Monitor%20 2011%20Update%20Master%20Word%20Document.pdf

Nutbrown, C., & Clough, P. (2009). Citizenship and inclusion in the early years: Understanding and responding to children's perspective on "belonging". *International Journal of Early Years Education*, 17(3), 191–206.

O'Brien, M., & Salonen, T. (2011). Child poverty and child rights meet active citizenship: A New Zealand and Sweden case study. *Childhood*, 18(2), 211–226.

Organisation for Economic Co-operation and Development. (OECD). (2011). *Society at a glance 2011: OECD social indicators.* Paris, France: Author. Retrieved from http://www.oecd.org/els/social/indicators/SAG

Restorative Schools. (2011). *Restorative conversations: The bookmark.* Retrieved from http://restorativeschools.org.nz/resources

Ridge, T. (2006). Childhood poverty: A barrier to social participation. In E. Tisdall, J. Davis, M. Hill, & A. Prout (Eds.), *Children, young people and social participation: Participation for what?* (pp. 23–28). Bristol, UK: The Policy Press.

Rigney, D. (2010). *The Matthew Effect: How advantage begets further advantage.* New York, NY: Colombia University Press.

Ritchie, J., Lockie, C., & Rau, C. (2011). He tatau pounamu: Considerations for an early childhood peace curriculum focusing on criticality, indigeneity, and an ethic of care, in Aotearoa New Zealand. *Journal of Peace Education*, 8(3), 333–352.

Smith, A. (2007). Children's rights and early childhood education: Links to theory and advocacy. *Australian Journal of Early Childhood*, 32(1), 1–8.

Thomas, N. (2007). Towards a theory of children's participation. *International Journal of Children's Rights*, 15, 199–218.

Thrupp, M. (2007). Education's "inconvenient truth": Part One—persistent middle class advantage. *New Zealand Journal of Teachers' Work*, 4(2), 77–78.

Thrupp, M. (2008). Education's "inconvenient truth": Part Two—the middle classes have too many friends in education. *New Zealand Journal of Teachers' Work*, 5(1), 54–62.

United Nations Committee on the Rights of the Child (UNCRC). (2011). *Consideration of reports submitted by States parties under Article 44 of the Convention*. Paris, France: United Nations.

Walden, C. (2011). *Monopoly games in the nursery: Community, inequalities and early childhood education*. Auckland: The Salvation Army Social Policy and Parliamentary Unit.

Wilkinson, R., & Pickett, K. (2010). *The spirit level: Why equality is better for everyone*. London, UK: Penguin.

CHAPTER 6

Speaking from the margins to the centre in early childhood initial teacher education

Gina Colvin, Darcey M. Dachyshyn and Jo Togiaso

There are a number of lessons I learned from my years at Jones Street Kindergarten[3]—lessons that I recall with some, albeit visceral, clarity. I learned that being a child among children can sometimes be a messy business, that learning can be joyous, children can feel alone amidst the chaos of other children, that there were rules to follow, and that teachers could be kind, but also cruel.

I also learned that there was such a word as "unfair" because I used it in a 4-year-old rage against a team of racist white early childhood teachers, none of whom had left me with any sense at all that I was anything but an aberration. At 4 years old, the ex-nuptial child of a Māori father and a Pākehā mother, I was able to name their racism and their prejudice because my mother (who never lied to me) saw that the only way to protect me was to give me the language to speak about this deeply complex social situation.

"Why don't they like me?" I asked my mother.

"Because you are half-caste, darling, and they don't like half-castes."

---

3 Name changed.

"Why don't they like half-castes Mum?"

"Because they're racist, sweetheart, which means they don't like some people because of the colour of their skin or the way they look. Not liking someone because of the way they look is a bad thing. Always remember that you are beautiful and clever, and you can do anything you want."

And so, although I was only 4 years old, my mother was forced to help me make sense of a divisive world to protect me from the possibility that I would accept my race or my half-casteness as my problem. She understood that it would be a problem for others, but I was under strict instructions to disregard their prejudices as a basis for questioning myself.

For me, a young child growing up in Christchurch, Aotearoa New Zealand, the more sober memories of my social life are characterised by the sense of my "race" or my "in-betweenness" preceding me. Living primarily with and around white folk, I was subject to their quips, sermons, totalising judgements—the "knowing gaze" about my "race" and the often-suffocating inability to escape from a predetermined course. It seemed that much of how I was to be understood at the level of the social had already been worked out.

My colour and my race, it appeared, were difficult for many white teachers to ignore. This was most evident during my social transgressions. The rapidity and force of white folks' responses to my misdemeanours once I started school suggested that the adults who were responsible for my education thought they knew me, and anticipated me on a level of which I was wholly unaware. It was this fabric of feeling that gave rise to my sense of disquiet, dis-ease, disequilibrium and displacement in education contexts. It was as if the circle had closed, with me on the outside, and that although there were important and magical things to be talked about at school, I was only permitted to look on as an outsider, as an observer of those conversations, never a participant.

I had to watch white teachers engage with white kids in a way that they never engaged with me because when they saw me they were drawing on an archive of interpretative repertoires and linguistic resources that came before me and over which I had no control. I had to daily watch the delight in their interactions with white kids; I had to hear the change in their tone of voice from impatience with me to delight with them. I saw their tolerance with white kids, which was intertwined with their expectation that moments of childish frustration with the lesson material would be overcome and success would follow. And I frequently experienced outbursts and taunts from my peers as they verbalised the unspoken antipathy that our teachers not so subtly directed at me.

I doubt that I would have been so sensitive to this kind of oppressiveness at school had my experience at kindergarten not been so brutalising, but I grew up understanding, with increasing acuity, that white teachers, while ostensibly well meaning, were at the same time frightening.

To think that minority children cannot read the cultural landscape, that they are not interested primarily in whether or not they are valued and loved as a member of a learning community, whether it is an early childhood centre or a school, is to underestimate the visceral awareness and emotive capacity of the child. It also underestimates the tangibility of the Anglo-normative practice that dominates education settings in Aotearoa New Zealand, particularly for children who have been pushed to the periphery.

So now when I see Māori children, I give them a special smile, reserved for all those Māori girls and boys who, through no fault of their own, have in one way or another asked themselves the question, "Why don't they like me?" I speak to them in Māori, even if they don't understand a word, because every time I have done this, their eyes say thank you, and they bask in this special language that we share through our ancestors. I laugh warmly and heartily at their silliness because I am just glad that they are alive and able to smile and look at the world with joy. I have made a deep, personal and unwavering commitment to Māori children because the places for them to go and see the shining and accepting eyes in the faces of their teachers have been and continue to be very limited.

Gina Colvin, age 44

Introduction

When, in 1996, the early childhood curriculum, *Te Whāriki*, was established, it became Aotearoa New Zealand's first bicultural and bilingual curriculum (Ministry of Education, 1996). The bicultural and bilingual focus of *Te Whāriki* signalled to the early childhood community, nationally and internationally, that dominant Western curriculum discourses must not be placed centre stage but should sit alongside other cultural perspectives. It represented and continues to represent the strong voices of both Māori and Pākehā. The introduction to the document makes this clear: "In early childhood settings, all children should be given the opportunity to develop knowledge and understanding of the cultural heritages of both partners to Te Tiriti o Waitangi" (Ministry of Education, 1996, p. 9).

This opportunity explicitly requires early childhood kaiako to support the use of Māori language and culture:

New Zealand is the home of Māori language and culture ... the curriculum in early childhood settings should promote te reo and ngā tikanga Māori, making them visible and affirming their value for children from all cultural backgrounds. (Ministry of Education, 1996, p. 42)

The curriculum also requires early childhood kaiako to give recognition to Māori ways of knowing, of making sense of the world and of respecting the natural environment. This recognition includes Māori people, places and artefacts, as well as activities, stories and events that have connections with the lives of tamariki Māori. It thus makes clear that these are an essential part of the curriculum for all children in early childhood settings. Traditional perspectives of early childhood predicated on a dominant Western discourse are thus rightfully counterbalanced in the curriculum by the foregrounding of Māori perspectives and "other voices" (Fleer, 2003).

Active demonstration of these cultural competencies has profound implications for early childhood teachers in Aotearoa New Zealand.

As May (2001) points out, the bicultural approach to curriculum that underpins *Te Whāriki* challenges kaiako familiar with the long-established practice in mainstream centres of providing children with play areas and offering them an established range of activities. Teachers, according to Ritchie (2003), fail to deliver a bicultural curriculum due to being ill equipped, viewing the curriculum as optional, and lacking in knowledge, confidence and competence. Also, Ritchie claims, settings are inevitably selective when formulating their programmes. As such, the inclusion of ngā tikanga and te reo Māori in the curriculum remains marginalised. These barriers help explain why, despite providing a framework of principles and strands that each early childhood setting can apply in its own unique way, many early childhood services find embracing and practising the spirit and intent of *Te Whāriki* problematic (May, 2001).

Similar concerns are evident in the New Zealand Teachers Council's decision, in 2007, to make demonstration of cultural competence a professional standard for graduating teachers and registered teachers working within Aotearoa New Zealand's education system. More specifically, the council's requirement called for kaiako to have enough knowledge of ngā tikanga and te reo Māori "to work effectively within the bicultural contexts of Aotearoa New Zealand ... [and to] have an understanding of education within the bicultural, multicultural, social, political, economic and historical contexts of Aotearoa New Zealand" (New Zealand Teachers Council, 2009).

However, procuring and exhibiting this understanding has posed a significant challenge for many teachers (Ritchie, 2007). This is not surprising given they belong to a profession that historically (and often explicitly) has been the engine room driving the formation of social hierarchies, the privileging of white colonial hegemonies, and the intergenerational transmission of ideologies (Zamudio, Bridgeman, & Rios, 2011).

The considerations just outlined make imperative the need for Aotearoa New Zealand early childhood kaiako to find ways of developing cultural competency when working with tamariki and whānau from culturally and linguistically diverse backgrounds, and also tamariki Māori and their whānau. This imperative is at the heart of our discussion in this chapter of what it means to be culturally competent in Aotearoa New Zealand in general, and in early childhood settings in particular.

Cultural competency requires kaiako not only to be inclusive of difference and diversity, but also to explicitly, consciously and productively draw on two different cultural traditions that have been historically oppositional and which continue to carry the traces of a deep-seated, intergenerational prejudice. It is one thing to include the newcomer (immigrant, refugee or 1.5 generation) minority child and his or her whānau into the community of an early childhood setting, and to honour and respect their cultural heritage, but it is quite another to negotiate who you are and what you do professionally as a teacher with respect for cultural competency. This is because, as we argue in this chapter, indigenous protest and politics have influenced the political terrain and have raised questions about race privilege.

To meaningfully address this situation, and to ensure that *Te Whāriki* can continue to be a catalyst for change towards cultural competency (Cullen, 2003), those of us who work within early childhood settings must critique our own practices and programmes within the parameters of how we are honouring Te Tiriti o Waitangi. Are we effectively incorporating te reo and tikanga Māori in everyday experiences? Do we understand the "world view" of tamariki and whānau from backgrounds different to our own? Are we constantly questioning who we are and what we do as teachers in this regard?

Understanding culture and cultural identity

Questions such as these both inform and aid exploration of what it means to be a culturally competent early childhood teacher. The meanings that are extracted draw on the notion that personal identity and collective identity are inextricably linked to culture, language and place (Steinbock, 1995). What then is culture? While many definitions exist, the simplicity of this definition—*culture is the everyday ways we live our lives*—serves as our focal point (Rogoff, 2003). Exotic aspects of cultural communities, such as dances, ethnic costumes, special foods and the like, are an aspect of culture. However, in our daily encounters with tamariki and whānau, it is the everyday ways we live our lives and thus engage in our encounters with others that serve to bind us together or divide us.

Alongside the view of culture as the everyday sits the view that, through these everyday encounters we derive our identities. In other words, we come to be and know who we are (Lave & Wenger, 1991; Wenger, 1999). This is the basis of sociocultural-historical theories (Göncü, 1999; Leontiev, 1981; Vygotsky, 1978, 1986; Wertsch, 1985, 1991). It is the people, places, things and experiences that we have encountered and continue to encounter that form our culture and that shape us. Furthermore, because the world we live in is constantly adapting and transforming, our culture and cultural identity are also continually changing. In our increasingly globalised world, encounters between different cultural influences and ways of living lead to individuals and communities adopting a variety of influences that result in *hybrid* identities; for example, Kiwi-Muslim, or Māori-Pākehā.

In the Aotearoa New Zealand context, the idea of Māori identity is shot through with complexity. While, on the one hand, anyone of Māori descent, irrespective of blood quantum, may claim Māori identity and therefore belonging, there is, for Māori, as a colonised indigenous people, more complexity to negotiate than simply that denoted by the assignment of a genetic heritage. Contemporary Māori identity includes the collective experience of white supremacist settler hegemonies. Māori identity comprises not only the habits of the everyday (including language, ritual and custom), but also the social and cultural adjustments and accommodations that were necessary because of colonial incursion.

Māori identity consists of the collective experience of language loss and the politics around revitalisation. It includes the collective experience of recent urbanisation and questionable government policies to manage that change. It includes an ongoing negotiation with the politics of representation and the need to manage the kinds of contested information that flies under the banner of *Māori* when we read a newspaper or turn on the television. If the "everyday" includes encountering racism, prejudice and the need to be cognisant of the effect of one's race on the dominant majority, then Māori identity and Māori culture must be understood as being constituted by a legacy of economic, social and political deprivation to much the same degree as it is informed by traditional practices (McIntosh, 2005).

Early childhood and the social construction of culture and identity

Young children have a significant role in mediating the formation of the hybridised identities that not only they but also their parents adopt (Dachyshyn & Kirova, 2008). Those of us working within early childhood contexts must heighten our understanding and practice of what it means to be culturally competent kaiako who are wise, empathic and open to diversity (Garmon, 2004). Only then can we provide spaces and places of belonging for all people. In addition to requiring kaiako to possess or cultivate a disposition that is inclusive and empathic, cultural competence in the Aotearoa New Zealand context calls on non-Māori teachers to be knowledgeable about Aotearoa New Zealand's historical, social and political context. It also asks them to be aware of their own constitution within a social arrangement that has privileged white settler hegemonies over successive generations of Māori ways of being and knowing, and that has continued to reproduce Anglo-normative practices in education settings (Hokowhitu, 2003).

The place of language is of special note within this discussion of culture and identity. Heidegger's (1971) premise that language is the "house of being" (p. 5) suggests that language is not simply something that is "nice to have", something that is helpful to communication. Language is what gives shape and substance to our world and what makes us who we are. Teachers often don't give due recognition to the complex linguistic and cultural reordering that children are forced to undertake when they move into educational contexts where the language spoken is not their own. It is therefore so much more than a temporary inconvenience when someone is in the midst of acquiring another language. Of children, we often say, "They are resilient; they pick up the language so quickly." To hold this view diminishes the loss of self that comes with the loss of language.

For newcomer children who have relocated to a cultural context that requires them to learn a new language, this time of being *in-between* is a time when even the things that are known become unfamiliar because it is in the naming that we know them (Kirova, 2006). Only as the language of the thing becomes familiar does the thing itself become familiar. Kirova suggests that families relocated to a cultural context where their home language is not widely spoken are forced to wonder (assuming that language is the house of being) "Which house do I choose to dwell in, and how do I maintain the language of my being?"

In our work with newcomer whānau, it is vital that we support them to maintain and grow their home language with their children. It is fair to say that it is impossible for every teacher in every early childhood setting to be able to do the work required to make sure that tamariki maintain their home language and culture. For that, whānau must take responsibility. We can, however, provide early childhood settings that legitimate and encourage home language and culture and thereby instil a message of pride and value in one's culture and identity (Dachyshyn & Kirova, 2011; Paradis, Kirova, & Dachyshyn, 2009).

While the need is present to honour and preserve home languages for newcomer families, there is an added imperative for those of us working within the Aotearoa New Zealand early childhood context (and, indeed, in any caregiving and teaching context), and that is to be part of efforts to revitalise te reo Māori and to acquire some proficiency in the language. Rather than having kaiako simply acknowledge te reo Māori as an official language of New Zealand, the New Zealand Teachers Council insists that registered teachers "demonstrate respect for the heritages, languages and cultures of both partners to the Treaty of Waitangi" (New Zealand Teachers Council, 2007).

Although there is some ambiguity in relation to the notion of *respect*, the criterion still asks for some demonstrable practice as an indicator of that respect. Thus, kaiako in Aotearoa New Zealand are required to learn and use te reo Māori and to be culturally proficient with the language by demonstrating that they understand not only the importance of te reo Māori but also have some facility with it. But over and above acknowledgement of home language is the need, within the Aotearoa New Zealand education system (as briefly noted above), to be part of a language revitalisation effort.

Finally, in turning to highlight the significance of *place* in the explication of culture and identity, we draw on Steinbock's (1995) explanation: "When we 'change places' or take up residence elsewhere, we do not simply leave the terrain behind. ... *The terrain attaches to the lived-body*" (p. 166, emphasis in original). In our work with tamariki and their whānau, we must recognise the deeply embedded influence of the places we each come from (Dachyshyn, 2012, in press). Today, when the movement of people between vastly different places has become increasingly common, early childhood settings are uniquely positioned to offer tamariki encounters with diversity as it is lived—in our bodies, not simply in the foods we eat and the holidays we celebrate.

Biculturalism, multiculturalism and interculturalism: Meanings and relationships

To further the discussion of what it means to become early childhood teachers who are culturally competent, we consider it necessary to differentiate between the terms "biculturalism", "multiculturalism" and "interculturalism". Education research and pedagogy has been dominated, over the last 30 years at least, by discourse focused on multiculturalism (Hage, 2002; Kirova, 2008). The result of this dominance is that cultural communities have often remained autonomous, isolated units on the margins of the dominant culture rather than an integral part of the cultural fabric of a nation. The term "interculturalism" offers a vision of dialogue and interchange such that all cultures and all individuals see themselves as continually shifting and hybridising "entities" who—together—constitute the culture of a nation, community, region. This is not to say that all people speaking and writing about multiculturalism and multicultural education are positioning ethnic groups as satellites on the borders of the dominant culture. Many scholars and pedagogues use the terms interchangeably (Grant & Portera, 2011). Perhaps, though, a change in terminology, from multiculturalism to interculturalism, might lead to a change in practice built on new thinking and new consciousness, and facilitate the development of more equitable societies.

Of particular note within this discussion is the use of the term "biculturalism" in Aotearoa New Zealand. In teacher education, and specifically among those in the field of early childhood education, many still struggle to differentiate between biculturalism and multiculturalism. For instance, as part of the ongoing professional development of staff at a New Zealand university, those driving the process called for contributions and ideas relating to the content and direction of teaching programmes for initial teacher education. With the aspiration for a degree modelling bicultural practice and recognition of Te Tiriti o Waitangi in mind, participants debated the following question: "Are we really sure about what bicultural practice looks like?" However, rather than allowing the academic staff involved to gain shared understandings about the nature of bicultural practice, the discussion highlighted diversity and complexity. Debate about the relationship between biculturalism and multiculturalism was particularly intense. For some, biculturalism sat alone and involved a different conversation than the broader discussions on multicultural/intercultural practice. For others, these ideas occupied the same discursive territory, and the pursuit of bicultural practice was understood to be at the expense of multiculturalism.

Three broad arguments appeared as participants shared their thoughts. At one end of the continuum there was a call for the idea of biculturalism to be replaced with the need to pursue rangatiratanga (sovereignty over all things Māori). Another strong argument revolved around the proposition that if Aotearoa New Zealand could practise biculturalism successfully, then good multicultural practice would follow. For the third "group", biculturalism occupied the same space as multiculturalism, and pursuing biculturalism meant eschewing an interest in non-Māori minority inclusion.

Each of these arguments elicits the possibility that the spaces we inhabit in relation to the question of what bicultural practice looks like range broadly across some highly contested discursive territory. May (2002) provides a very useful approach for disaggregating the ideas of multiculturalism and biculturalism from each other. Simply put, bicultural practice arises out of the implementation of interrelated legislation specifically aimed at protecting a national minority (Māori) for whom Aotearoa New Zealand is a home of origin, and for whom a colonial incursion has meant an intergenerational encounter with some deleterious circumstances. The legislation includes the Māori Language Act 1975, the Treaty of Waitangi Act 1975, the State-Owned Enterprises Act 1986 and various aspects of common law. Together, these create a corpus of policy and regulatory guidelines that ostensibly work to invoke participatory, protective and partnership imperatives on the part of the Crown and Māori (specifically, iwi).

Multicultural practice, however, involves a different body of policies and regulations that have mostly come out of human rights legislation in Aotearoa New Zealand. This corpus works towards ensuring that social fairness and justice prevail and that diversity is valued and protected, specifically for ethnic and newcomer minorities who require some extra protection from the vagaries of the dominant majority (May, 2002). Multicultural practice is therefore done in addition to bicultural practice, and it also raises the obligation for multicultural practice in education contexts to be bicultural.

Culturally competent early childhood teaching: Responding to the Aotearoa New Zealand context

Racist education practices in Aotearoa New Zealand have historically worked to serve and naturalise white colonial hegemony and privilege (Simon, 2000). The literature suggests that white settler societies, including those in this country, are awash with systems of ideas that work to reinforce and maintain particular relations, boundaries and exclusions across and among several of its member groups (Colvin, 2009; Razack, 2002; Stasiulis & Yuval-Davis, 1995). These ideas are reproduced in education settings in order to sustain a social hierarchy that affords particular benefits and privileges to the dominant majority. Through our efforts, as kaiako in early childhood settings, to understand that racist practices work to shape a hierarchy of human value, we might be well placed to rethink and disrupt the dominance of these social meanings.

But it is not enough to establish that Aotearoa New Zealand's white colonial hegemony exists in education settings and to examine the consequences of white privilege that are daily visited upon *othered* children within these settings (for a discussion on *othering*, see Ashcroft, Griffiths, & Tiffin, 1998, p. 171). We need to talk about these issues within a clear historical and social context that seeks to account for how and why the white colonial account in Aotearoa New Zealand education came to be normalised, and how and why it continues to have currency.

Too often in our work with tamariki and whānau with cultural and linguistic backgrounds different from our own, we see those differences as deficiencies (Bomer, Dworin, May, & Semingson, 2008). We see the one who is *differently arranged* as needy and incapable, as lacking skills and knowledge (Fleer, 2003). It is time to turn that thinking around and see differences as gifts, as "funds of knowledge" (González, Moll, & Amanti, 2005), and as opportunities to engage with people, places, things and events that make us more fully human (Smith, 2003, 2006).

Furthermore, our approach to education and to our work with tamariki and whānau is most often that of *doing*, of getting things done, of doing the right thing, of taking precise action, of looking for set outcomes based on certain inputs. Then, if we do not get the results we are looking for, we might blame something or someone. In reality, life is messy, and teaching is highly complex—there are no right answers, there are no best practices, there are no right ways of doing things. Rather, our task as intercultural early childhood kaiako is to live mindfully, presently and openly in each and every moment and encounter that come our way. It is a mind-set, a way of *being* (Fromm, 2005) with people and with oneself, rather than a set of actions, that this chapter invites you to engage in.

The point that we are emphasising here is that, for those of us involved in education, the territory is highly contested and looks set to remain so for some time. However, this situation need not be a reason for paralysis or retreat. The very paradoxes that exist between us are an indication not only of the presence of a pervasive cultural hegemony, but also of a rich terrain that holds our conflicts and contradictions in a field of potentially positive tension.

We have purposefully named this "a field of potentially positive tension" because it is our argument that the confluence of the tensions directed towards resolving our own uncertainties will yield richer discourse than will simply aiming for a kind of banal and unassuming commonality. Consensus is probably less desirable than the risk-taking and boldness associated with pursuing a course in which there is expressed uncertainty and doubt. It is the nature of intellectual work that calls us to be in a kind of incessant conversation with one another. Traditionally, this dialogue takes place in the sympathetic silos of the academic journal, which characteristically breeds its own kind of intellectual siblings. All the while, academics, teachers and families in the same hallways, departments, early childhood settings, schools and communities avoid the opportunities to converse questioningly and wonderingly with those whose opinions they find hard to justify or comprehend.

Conclusions

This chapter has rested on the understanding that, within Aotearoa New Zealand, and within post-colonial countries generally, the white English-speaking middle-class population dominates society, and those who do not fit that demographic are subjected to racism, be that blatant or systemic. This is a difficult pill to swallow for those who are of the dominant culture—a harder pill still to swallow for those who are the marginalised (Dachyshyn, 2007).

In the final analysis, white colonial discourse in Aotearoa New Zealand's early childhood settings and school classrooms has been about the heirarchisation, ascendancy, power, control, domination and authority of whiteness in Aotearoa New Zealand in the face of a contested incursion. However, because the marginalisation of others in Aotearoa New Zealand has occurred as an unfortunate consequence of white hegemony, white hegemony is the social and cultural site that requires interrogation; continually examining mythologised versions of Aotearoa New Zealand history in the hopes that setting the record straight might encourage better *race relations* is not. It is time we moved beyond revising ethnocentric accounts of Aotearoa New Zealand's colonisation. We need to engage not with what was poorly written, but to ask why these accounts had currency historically, and what work they are doing in contemporary Aotearoa New Zealand (see Colvin, 2009).

The essential matter to consider—if one holds to the premise within sociocultural-historical theories that we are who we are because of where we come from in terms of the people, places, things and events that have shaped us—is that if we have been raised in a colonial country, we cannot help but be who we are. Because we have been immersed in a hierarchical context, where the white English-speaking middle class dominates, we tend to traverse our way through that "reality" with blinkers on. Moreover, when the society in which we live is working well for us, why see any problems with it? Why think that things need to change? It is only when we ask and debate the questions that allow us to emerge from that clouded vision and to see the world through different eyes that we can begin to see the inequities that exist. In our work with tamariki and whānau from a multitude of backgrounds, it behoves us to understand the lived experience of those who are different from ourselves. To do so is to begin the journey towards creating places and spaces of true wellbeing and belonging for all.

References

Ashcroft, B., Griffiths, G., & Tiffin, H. (1998). *Key concepts in post-colonial studies.* London, UK: Routledge.

Bomer, R., Dworin, J. E., May, L., & Semingson, P. (2008). Miseducating teachers about the poor: A critical analysis of Ruby Payne's claims about poverty. *Teachers College Record, 110*(12), 2497–2531.

Colvin, G. (2009). *The soliloquy of whiteness: Colonial discourse and the New Zealand settler press, 1839–1872.* Unpublished doctoral thesis, University of Canterbury.

Cullen, J. (2003). The challenge of *Te Whāriki*: Catalyst for change? In J. Nuttall (Ed.), *Weaving Te Whāriki: Aotearoa New Zealand's early childhood curriculum document in theory and practice* (pp. 269–296). Wellington: NZCER Press.

Dachyshyn, D. M. (2007). Refugee families with preschool children: Adjustment to life in Canada. In L. Adam & A. Kirova (Eds.), *Global migration and education: Schools, children, and families.* Mahwah, NJ: Lawrence Erlbaum.

Dachyshyn, D. M. (2012, in press). Children dwelling in the absence of home. *Indo-Pacific Journal of Phenomenology,* Special Edition 12 (May).

Dachyshyn, D. M., & Kirova, A. (2008). Understanding childhoods in-between: Sudanese refugee children's transition from home to preschool. *Research in Comparative and International Education, 3*(3), 281–294.

Dachyshyn, D. M., & Kirova, A. (2011). Classroom challenges in developing an intercultural early learning program for refugee children. *Alberta Journal of Education Research, 57*(2), 219–232.

Fleer, M. (2003). Early childhood education as an evolving "community of practice" or as lived "social reproduction": Researching the "taken-for-granted". *Contemporary Issues in Early Childhood, 4*(1), 64–79.

Fromm, E. (2005). *To have or to be?* London, UK: Continuum.

Garmon, M. A. (2004). Changing preservice teachers' attitudes/beliefs about diversity. *Journal of Teacher Education, 55*(3), 201–213.

Göncü, A. (Ed.). (1999). *Children's engagement in the world.* Cambridge, UK: Cambridge University Press.

González, N., Moll, C. M., & Amanti, C. (2005). *Funds of knowledge: Theorizing practices in households, communities, and classrooms.* Mahwah, NJ: Lawrence Erlbaum Associates.

Grant, C. A., & Portera, A. (Eds.). (2011). *Intercultural and multicultural education: Enhancing global interconnectedness.* New York, NY: Routledge.

Hage, G. (2002). *Arab-Australians today: Citizenship and belonging*. Carlton, VIC: Melbourne University Press.

Heidegger, M. (1971). *On the way to language*. New York, NY: HarperCollins.

Hokowhitu, B. (2003). "Physical beings": Stereotypes, sport and the "physical education" of New Zealand Māori. *Culture, Sport, Society, 6*(2), 192–218.

Kirova, A. (2006). Moving childhoods: Young children's lived experiences of being between languages and cultures. In L. Adams & A. Kirova (Eds.), *Global migration and education: Schools, children and families* (pp. 185–198). Mahwah, NJ: Lawrence Erlbaum Associates.

Kirova, A. (2008). Critical and emerging discourses in multicultural education literature: A review. *Canadian Ethnic Studies, 40*(1), 101–124.

Lave, J., & Wenger, E. (1991). *Situated learning: Legitimate peripheral participation*. Cambridge, UK: Cambridge University Press.

Leontiev, A. N. (1981). *Problems of the development of the mind*. Moscow, USSR: Progress Publishers.

May, H. (2001). *Politics in the playground: The world of early childhood in postwar New Zealand*. Wellington: Bridget Williams Books/New Zealand Council for Educational Research.

May, S. (2002). Accommodating multiculturalism and biculturalism in Aotearoa New Zealand: Implications for language education. *Waikato Journal of Education, 8*, 5–26.

McIntosh, T. (2005). Māori identities: Fixed, fluid, and forced. In J. Liu, T. McCreanor, T. McIntosh, & T. Teaīwa (Eds.), *New Zealand identities: Departures and destinations*. Wellington: Victoria University Press.

Ministry of Education. (1996). *Te whāriki: He whāriki mātauranga mō ngā mokopuna o Aotearoa: Early childhood curriculum*. Wellington: Learning Media.

New Zealand Teachers Council. (2007). *Graduating teacher standards*. Wellington: Author. Retrieved from http://www.teacherscouncil.govt.nz/te/gts

New Zealand Teachers Council. (2009). *Registered teacher criteria*. Wellington: Author. Retrieved from www.teacherscouncil.govt.nz/rtc/index.stm

Paradis, J., Kirova, A., & Dachyshyn, D. M. (2009). *Working with young children who are learning English as a new language*. Edmonton, Alberta, Canada: Alberta Education.

Razack, S (Ed). (2002). *Race, space and the law: Unmapping white settler society*. Toronto, Ontario, Canada: Between the Lines.

Ritchie, J. (2003). One context, two outcomes: A comparison of *Te Whāriki* and the New Zealand curriculum framework. In J. Nuttall (Ed.), *Weaving Te*

Whāriki: Aotearoa New Zealand's early childhood curriculum document in theory and practice (pp. 79–109). Wellington: NZCER Press.

Ritchie, J. (2007). Thinking Otherwise: "Bicultural" hybridities in early childhood education in Aotearoa/New Zealand. *Childrenz Issues: Journal of the Children's Issues Centre, 11*(1), 37–41. Retrieved from http://search.informit.com.au/documentSummary;dn=367460233396127; res=IELHSS

Rogoff, B. (2003). *The cultural nature of human development.* New York, NY: Oxford University Press.

Simon, J. (2000). Education policy change: Historical perspectives. In J. Marshal, E. Coxon, K. Jenkins, & A. Jones (Eds.), *Politics, policy, pedagogy: Education in Aotearoa / New Zealand* (pp. 25–63). Palmerston North: Dunmore.

Smith, D. G. (2003). Preface: Some thoughts on living in-between. In E. Hasebe-Lundt & W. Hurren (Eds.), *Curriculum intertext: Place/language/pedagogy* (pp. xv–xvii). New York, NY: Peter Lang.

Smith, D. G. (2006). Troubles with the sacred canopy: Global citizenship in a season of great untruth. In G. H. Richardson (Ed.), *Troubling the canon of citizenship education* (pp. 124–135). New York, NY: Peter Lang.

Stasiulis, D., & Yuval-Davis, N. (Eds.). (1995). *Unsettling settler societies: Articulations of gender, race, ethnicity and class.* London, UK: Sage.

Steinbock, A. J. (1995). *Home and beyond: Generative phenomenology after Husserl.* Evanston, IL: Northwestern University Press.

Vygotsky, L. S. (1978). *Mind in society: The development of higher psychological processes.* Cambridge, MA: Harvard University Press.

Vygotsky. L. S. (1986). *Thought and language.* Cambridge, MA: The MIT Press.

Wenger, E. (1999). *Communities of practice: Learning, meaning, and identity.* Cambridge, UK: Cambridge University Press.

Wertsch, J. V. (1985). *Culture, communication, and cognition: Vygotskian perspectives.* New York, NY: Cambridge University Press.

Wertsch, J. V. (1991). *Voices of the mind: A sociocultural approach to mediated action.* Cambridge, MA: Harvard University Press.

Zamudio, M., Bridgeman, J. L., & Rios, F. (2011). *Critical race theory matters: Education and ideology.* New York, NY: Routledge.

CHAPTER 7

The construction of disadvantage for boys and men in Aotearoa New Zealand early childhood education: The gender debates continue

Alexandra C. Gunn

Teachers are convinced boys need different equipment, approaches, activities, even without considering in what ways boys are disadvantaged or that their new strategies are simply reinforcing one way.

So said a colleague as she and I talked in late 2009 about a conference address I had been invited to give. The requested focus of my talk was teachers' pedagogies in relation to current so-called issues of *boys' educational needs*. My colleague's comment came to represent the nub of my address: how had we come to expect that boys need special pedagogies in early childhood education, and what effects might this expectation have on our thinking about and doing of everyday practice as early childhood teachers?

In this chapter—and motivated by the need to address further the persistent construction of disadvantage in relation to boys and male teachers in Aotearoa New Zealand early childhood education—I broaden my keynote-focused analysis of the situation for boys to an analysis encompassing all tamariki and kaiako. Within this framework I consider recently deployed discourses on boys' underachievement and the feminised workforce in schooling and in early childhood education.

The relationship of these discourses to the notion of disadvantage is noted as I contemplate how such discourses might be working at the local level to open up and shut down opportunities for gender diversity and inclusive education. I write to draw attention to the ways these discourses construct men, boys, women and girls, and to unsettle any idea that there is an *essential* or *proper* way to be boy- or man-friendly as a teacher. I argue for resistance to such limiting discourses and for the development of practices that are equity-friendly and that engage with gender diversity. Framing difference as positive, I take up equity discourses from Aotearoa New Zealand's early childhood curriculum *Te Whāriki* (Ministry of Education, 1996) in an effort to reorient thinking away from the problems that early childhood education is assumedly posing for boys and men and towards this question: What is fair for different boys, men, girls and women who are engaged in early childhood education?

My position on gender

Before going further, I consider it important to establish my "theoretical" position on gender and to set it within various constructs of gender. My position is informed by feminist poststructuralism. At the practical level, this means that I do not ascribe to a theory of gender that posits it as innate, immutable and fixed. Nor do I conflate biological sex with gender. Rather, I take a lead from poststructural scholars and writers on gender, such as Davies (1989a, 1989b), MacNaughton (2000), Walkerdine (1981) and Weedon (1987), who recognise gender as inherently ambiguous and achieved through repeated performances of gendered acts. From this position, being masculine and being feminine is seen as occurring in the context of social processes that gain prominence in particular sociohistorical and sociopolitical times. What it means to be legitimately masculine and feminine is therefore subject to change, which makes our "doing" of gender a very complex "action".

Manifest through what we do rather than as an element of who we are, our gendered performances become coherent and stable enough over time for us to be (more often than not) recognised as one gender or another. The perspective recognises gender diversity rather than fixing on a non-contradictory and narrow gender identity. This view, with respect to inclusive education, opens up possibilities to engage with difference and with equity given that children's encounters with gender, particularly in their early years, are plentiful and varied.

Several theoretical positions have been used over the years to explore, explain and describe gender. In my experience, the feminist poststructural view is one that Aotearoa New Zealand teachers and student teachers in early childhood education rarely subscribe to. Dominant within my own histories within early childhood education, and still frequently espoused when I ask students in tertiary education what gender is and how it occurs, is the explanation that gender is typically an outcome of biological processes or social conditioning.

These biological and social theories of gender, each of which has a long history within developmental psychology, are somewhat similar. The biological argument positions gender as an innate and naturally unfolding characteristic of one's personhood that accounts for and relies on a binary distinction of two different sexes—male and female. The socialisation perspective builds from this understanding to assert that, across the natural biological divide, gender is somewhat flexible and therefore responsive to teaching and to learning. Thus, we can resist traditional and stereotypical gender development by actively having modelled for us and learning different ways to be male and female (Davies, 1989a).

These dominant views on gender are essentialising—that is, they are reliant on the idea that there is a universal set of characteristics of masculinity and femininity which all women and men, regardless of culture or historical context, share—and, as mentioned already, they are reliant on binary understandings of gender for their coherence. Binary oppositions were noted by French philosopher and linguist Jacques Derrida (1976, 1978) as a feature of Western languages. Within his dichotomy, gender relies on the division of masculine and feminine, male and female, boy and girl in order to generate meanings about each of those terms. Each term sits in opposition to the other and is mutually exclusive: the essential meaning of being a boy or a man can be discerned by referencing its binary pair or opposite (girl or woman). The meaning of boy, then, is not girl, the meaning of man is not woman, and being masculine does not involve being feminine. This binary thinking is, according to Davies (1994, p. 8), "absolutely fundamental to the maintenance of the male/female dualism". As I and colleague Glenda MacNaughton argue elsewhere (e.g., Gunn & MacNaughton, 2007; MacNaughton, 2000), it is limiting with respect to engaging with gender diversity and equity in early childhood education.

I maintain that if we are to engage with equity and to practise inclusivity in relation to gender, then we must broaden our understandings of gender beyond such concepts. Engaging with gender diversity provides one means of thinking differently. Through a gender diversity lens, we can open ourselves to the possibility of viewing genders as multiple, and acknowledge, therefore, the existence of genders beyond the binary boy/girl. We can also view gender as fluid relative to time, place and culture, and therefore as inherently ambiguous and changeable.

Opening ourselves up to these perspectives does not necessarily mean actively seeking to reject all expressions of gender that evoke the gender binary or gender essentialism. Rather, this action enables us to recognise that such performances of gender are only some of the ways gender might be expressed by an individual at a given point in time. And if we do acknowledge diversity with respect to gender, then I think we are more likely to recognise when binary thinking or gender essentialism works to an individual's detriment, and to be sensitive to the ways in which gender constructions are expected of or imposed on tamariki, others and ourselves.

Engaging with equity means, by definition, treating people differently to ensure fair outcomes: gender diversity *recognises* difference. In recent times, however, dominant gender discourses in schooling and in early childhood education have done anything but this. Later in the chapter, I illustrate how.

Gender discourses, subject positions and inclusive education

According to Foucault (1969), discourses exist as statements within a single system or formation that combine, as Alsop, Fitzsimons and Lennon (2002, p. 82) explain, to "carry with them norms for behaviour, standards of what counts as desirable and undesirable, proper and improper". One may speak of discourses as "identified by the particular way in which they represent and construct the person" (Burr, 1995, p. 142), and they can be observed in and through the development and maintenance of particular practices, modes of exchange and constructed truths (Gergen, 1999). According to Davies (1989b), the discursive practices that we engage in work to constitute the self at any given point of time:

> ... discursive practices are not just an external constraint (or potentiation), they also provide the conceptual framework, the psychic patterns, the emotions through which each individual takes themselves up as male or female and through which they privately experience themselves in relation to the social world. (p. 235)

The idea of constructing the individual or, more accurately, of constructing subject positions that individuals come to occupy within discourse, has consequences for inclusion. This is because the construction of what counts as normal, or desirable or proper (and therefore as *not*) in relation to the individual, is embedded in discourse. For instance, as children learn the cultural conventions of gender that permeate the sociohistorical context in which they live, they take up or resist particular constructions. Repeated performances of some constructions marginalise other constructions as children and adults position themselves and are positioned in relation to these. We learn the conventions for so-called normal or proper forms of gender through these processes and, in doing so, simultaneously learn the opposite. Typically, constructions that rely on the gender binary of masculine/feminine are taken for granted. Only when they are disrupted in some way is our attention drawn to them. What we as kaikao need to ask ourselves with respect to dominant gender discourses are questions such as these:

- Should we ignore or disrupt their normalising effects?
- Is the way in which a dominant discourse constructs boys, men, women and girls fair?
- Who gains from the construction?
- Who does not?
- Is this something—given the equity concerns of our curriculum— that we might wish to perpetuate?

There will, of course, always be dominant discourses at work. What is an important action for us, however, is to recognise that it is our analysis of and responses to those discourses that can facilitate or limit inclusion.

Dominant gender discourses in Aotearoa New Zealand early childhood education

When I began working in early childhood education in the 1980s, gender concerns in this area of educational provision and research in Aotearoa New Zealand centred on *equality of opportunity* for girls.

Scholars studied teachers' actions and children's play patterns, noticing where boys dominated areas of the programme and, where it was thought necessary, encouraging girls to play (Halliday & McNaughton, 1982; McMillan, 1978; Meade & Staden, 1985; Smith, 1985). This thinking made its way into *Te Whāriki* (Ministry of Education, 1996), which included goals and outcomes related to gender equity (see, for example, the outcomes and examples related to the first goal of the contribution/mana tangata strand).[4]

However, as I and my colleagues moved into the 1990s, some of the dominant 1980s thinking about gender started to change: equality of opportunity for girls began to be framed as *detrimental for boys*. Weaver-Hightower (2003, p. 472) calls this growing international (and national) concern about an underclass of uneducated and underachieving males the "boy turn", a term exemplifying the changing shape of discourses about gender occurring at this time (see also Barker, 1997; Burman, 2005; Titus, 2004). For the purposes of this chapter, however, I focus on just two of the dominant gender discourses in Aotearoa New Zealand relating to the boy turn. The first is boys' underachievement, and the second is the feminised teacher workforce.

To contextualise the deployment of these discourses with respect to early childhood, I begin with a brief genealogy of them (Foucault, 1977) in relation to schooling. I then consider how and why they have come to prominence in early childhood education.

---

4 It is possible to critique the equality of opportunity campaign on the basis of its deployment of essentialising discourses of gender. It is also possible to read differently the deployment of such discourses in relation to that campaign given it occurred within a social system in which men did (and still do in the broader sense) dominate. Even though the gender pay gap in Aotearoa New Zealand is diminishing (Ministry of Women's Affairs, 2011), women continue to experience material disadvantage in Aotearoa New Zealand society by virtue of their gender. Thus, even though on the one hand this chapter critiques an essentialising perspective per se, in its sociohistorical context we are able to comprehend how such a view was of use at the time in resisting institutional oppressions resulting from patriarchy.

Underachieving boys

Before being deployed in the context of early childhood education, the discourse of underachieving boys was made relevant to Aotearoa New Zealand schooling. This discourse arose when questions about the shape of boys' achievement in Western education systems began to be raised internationally. The brief genealogy and discourse analysis of the texts that follows is by no means the only possible reading of the documents and events described.[5] In this case, I want to demonstrate the conditions and context that helped give rise to discourses of disadvantage in relation to boys' and men's engagement in schooling and early childhood education in this country.

In the late 1990s, Aotearoa New Zealand's Education Review Office (ERO)[6] began looking at the relative achievement of boys and girls in secondary school. Concerns that girls were outperforming boys against most measures of achievement were raised when School Certificate[7] results showed, over time, a disparity between boys' and girls' success at school, with that disparity favouring girls' achievement. ERO's subsequent report on the matter, *The Achievement of Boys* (ERO, 1999), began by noting that not all boys and girls conformed to "gender types" and that not all boys were experiencing failure at school. However, ERO drew heavily on gender essentialism to advance its argument that a "pattern of underachievement" existed for boys, and that this pattern would have "serious consequences, both for boys themselves and for society at large" (ERO, 1999, p. 7).

In line with its essentialist frame, the authors of the report went on to argue that boys and girls learn differently. In order to maximise the educational success of boys and of girls, different teaching styles

---

5 Discourse analysis seeks to make visible multiple readings of a text to show how constructed and partial the truths we hold to can be (MacNaughton, 1998).

6 ERO is a government agency analogous to a school inspectorate.

7 This was the then nationally ascribed qualification that most students sat for at the end of their third year of high school.

were needed to work effectively with the two genders: "there is evidence that boys and girls learn and respond in different ways and achieve best with different teaching styles" (ERO, 1999, p. 8), the report said. These are not arguments advanced in the agency's most recent publication on boys' achievement (ERO, 2008).

Compounding the construction of schooling as problematic for boys, ERO presented evidence in its 1999 report of boys' over-representation in special education, truancy and suspension statistics. They also cited a study that posited boys' classroom behaviour as an impediment to their learning. The "feminine environment" within schools was likewise noted as a factor contributing to boys' "bad behaviour" at school. As a remedy to this state of affairs, and as an obvious response to the concerns of underachievement, the report's authors suggested "increasing the number of men in teaching and the number of male role models in schools" (ERO, 1999, p. 10).

Thus, the beginnings of an officially sanctioned discourse of *boy-friendly pedagogies* that would respond to the problem of boys' underachievement entered our education vernacular. It paved the way for kaiako in early childhood education, such as those referred to in this chapter's opening quote, to deem it necessary to take up particular pedagogies and to provide particular teachers so as to respond successfully to the plight of those disadvantaged.

Two years on from publication of the ERO report, the New Zealand Association of Boys' Schools launched a large-scale initiative to further explore the now established problem of boys' underachievement and disadvantage. In 2001 the Association invited former prison warden Celia Lashlie to undertake a project looking at the special qualities of boys. The purpose was to ascertain what boys' unique needs might be (the essence of being male) and to hypothesise with boys and men involved in single-sex secondary education about what making a good man in Aotearoa New Zealand's 21st century might look like (Lashlie, 2004). The account of mainstream education that emerged from the project also claimed that schooling was failing boys. It advocated that boys needed special teaching strategies and that they needed teachers of a particular kind (that is, men) if their disadvantage within the Aotearoa New Zealand education system was to be countered.

In 2003 a New Zealand National Party policy discussion paper on education claimed that New Zealand was facing a "crisis" in boys' educational achievement (Smith, 2003). Noting the success of the Girls Can Do Anything campaign of the late 20th century, the paper argued for a similar strategy to target boys' education, and also for a commission of inquiry into the crisis. The Ministry of Education responded the following year by establishing a taskforce charged with examining boys' achievement and identifying programmes that worked well for boys (Mallard, 2004). The taskforce's focus was to establish evidence of what could be considered effective teaching practices for boys at school.

An outcome of the initiative was the development of the current *Success for Boys* portal on tki.org (Ministry of Education, 2011). Despite the web page beginning with the declaration that "most boys are doing well at school"—a statement which, at face value, resists a homogenising approach to boys' education—the overall implication of the site and its content is clear: mainstream education must change if it is to counter the lack of educational success facing boys in Aotearoa New Zealand.

At the discursive level, Celia Lashlie's writing, the Ministry taskforce's efforts and the outcomes of other initiatives worked to institutionalise the notion that boys were or are disadvantaged and therefore underachieving in mainstream Aotearoa New Zealand education. The reasons (whether implicitly or explicitly voiced) underpinning this notion embody gender essentialism: boys are different and unique; they therefore need special teaching styles and particular kinds of teachers if their disadvantage in school is to be overcome. In the context of the broader boy turn, it is understandable how the claim that teachers must engage in specific kinds of practices and pedagogies can arise. And given that reasons for the disadvantage are based on gender-essentialist understandings, it is easy to see how such thinking can become generalised to early childhood education. For, in our field, the same messages have been perpetuated, albeit from a slightly different angle.

The feminised early childhood workforce

Publication of the report *Men at Work: Sexism in Early Childhood Education* (Farquhar, Cablk, Buckingham, Butler, & Ballantyne, 2006) and the release of a current affairs item on national television related to this report soon after (Skinner, 2006) saw several challenging claims made about the plight of men within early childhood education. The claims, at their most basic level, argued for the existence of a sexist workforce in early childhood education. Proof was held to be the low numbers of male teachers in the field, the lack of retention of those men who had entered it, and poor recruitment practices with respect to men on the part of the Ministry of Education and employer groups (Farquhar et al., 2006). The report's executive summary, for example, made the following claims.

- "The early childhood workforce seems stuck in the 1970s family model" (p. iii), with children's placement in "almost exclusively female" childcare environments and "their contact with positive male role models" reduced (p. iii).
- The workforce composition is sexist because early childhood teaching is not open to men, and this, associated with the fact that "talented women" are attracted to careers other than teaching, places young children at a "greater risk of substandard care and education" (p. iv).
- There are thus "negative consequences of the early childhood profession … continuing to be a strongly protected woman's one" (p. iv).

- "It is an embarrassment to New Zealand" (p. iv) that we have so few men teaching in early childhood education and that we have yet to substantially debate the issue.

The supposed thrust of the report—that recruiting men into early childhood teaching in Aotearoa is difficult, as is retaining them once there—is diminished in my mind because both the framing of the executive summary and the raft of other claims and assertions in the report itself evoke gender essentialism. The points noted above, for instance, can be read as: tamariki (read especially boys), it seems, are limited by being cared for and educated primarily by women in centre-based or group settings; tamariki (read especially boys) are seemingly missing out on the chance to be taught about gender from men as well as from women; and men are being denied the opportunity to act as gender role models for tamariki (read especially boys).

The comments about *role models* in particular reveal essentialist gender discourses at work: a socialisation perspective on gender is to the fore. Furthermore, the early childhood workforce is posited as *closed to* and *strongly protected from* men. This makes the field not only unfair for men but, it is claimed, also *risky* for children. Finally, the assertion that the field has thus far not substantially debated the issue of why so few men teach in it construes as current and ongoing the identified risks and inequities "facing" actual and potential male kaiako. When analysed discursively, this initial framing of the report in the executive summary establishes a dominant construction of disadvantage for men and boys in early childhood education.

In the body of the report, and after an initial "statistical overview" (pp. 3–5) of data from teacher-led early childhood services about the number of men teaching in them, the report presents six main reasons for the low number and declining proportion of male to female child-care teachers in Aotearoa New Zealand. Again we see evocation of the notion of male disadvantage.

First, both early childhood education and child care are claimed to have been sites for feminist activism since the 1970s and, as part of this, for "freeing women from childcare responsibilities in the home and increasing women's participation in paid work" (p. 5). The implication seems to be that this feminist activism has been, and is still, limiting to men's participation. Thus, women's right to work is construed as detrimental to and for men, in part because it leaves men somehow displaced.

Second, an argument about child care being "commonly viewed" (p. 5) as an extension of the mother's role is put forward. A study is cited in which a father reports his involvement in early childhood education as being constrained by "being with a lot of women ... its [*sic*] going into a setting where you're being surrounded by women" (Kahn, cited in Farquhar et al., 2006, p. 5). Here, men are positioned as easily troubled by being *surrounded by women*, and women are constructed as *dominating and overpowering*. A perception that women are "doing a perfectly good job" (p. 6) in child care is later argued as the third reason for the female-dominated workforce: the "door [is] shut on male entry into the early childhood profession" (p. 6).

The fourth and fifth reasons given for why so few men choose to become early childhood kaiako are said to be related to the possibility of them being suspected homosexuals and/or potential abusers of children (whereas all women are construed as *safe*). While these ideas counter, to some extent, the feminised early childhood workforce discourse, they still perpetuate the notion of male disadvantage in early childhood education. Finally, the profession is construed as a "low-pay and low-status occupation" (p. 7), presenting additional reasons why men do not teach in the field.

These six main reasons are stated as facts—as "the main reasons why childcare teaching is female dominated and what this means" (p. 5). The authors work persuasively and officially to construct men as actually or potentially disadvantaged from seeking work or actually working within early childhood education, and tamariki (again read boys) are construed as disadvantaged by this lack.

Discussing constructions of genders: Implications for inclusion

The construction of disadvantage for boys and for men is readily achieved when gender discourses of underachieving boys and a feminised teacher workforce are in play. These discourses, which open up subject positions for boys, men, girls and women to occupy, provide a conceptual framework through which we privately and publicly experience one another and ourselves in the social world.

Martino (2008) calls the recent *intensification* of interest in masculinities in young children's education part of a "broader cultural project of re-masculinization" (p. 192). He notes that fears of emasculation have repeatedly arisen throughout history and resulted in some sort of backlash against women. Thinking of my own teacher subjectivity, for instance, I am constructed through the underachieving boys' discourse as inadequate for meeting the full needs of any tamaiti I may teach. By virtue my gender, the discourse posits me as less able than a male colleague to recognise and respond effectively to the special characteristics of tamariki tāne. The discourse simultaneously constructs my male colleagues as more able to address such needs. It also positions me as a kaiako unable to expose tamariki to a range of ways of being masculine or feminine. Because the boy children with whom I might work in the context of an early childhood setting are perceived as unlikely to receive sufficient opportunities to learn how to be "proper" boys, the discourse constructs tamariki tāne as non-agentic in relation to learning about gender, and as disadvantaged should the setting be devoid of male teachers.

In relation to the discourse of the feminised teaching profession, I am construed as actively gate-keeping my profession to the detriment of my teaching peers, a construction that refuses to recognise the successes of men who do quality work in early childhood education. It also sees me, as a female kaiako, as limiting the range of gender models for children. Again, it fails to recognise the multiple ways children and adults experience and practise gender diversely in their everyday lives. Tamariki, for instance, see and interact with a range of men outside of the early childhood setting; they experience different masculinities and femininities through shared experiences with their peers, through their encounters with media and, in their own experience of—if not struggles with—gendered practices.

In this chapter, there has been space for me to draw attention to only a few examples of the constructions invoked by these dominant discourses, but they serve to illustrate how taken-for-granted assumptions in everyday practices can arise. Thus, "teachers [*become*] convinced boys need different equipment/approaches/activities, even".

If we unproblematically accept the ways such discourses position us, we can find ourselves caught up in a tangle of relations and relationships that actively encourage us to act in so-called normal or proper ways, even when we find these questionable. I suspect that the kaiako my colleague referred to in the introductory quote to this chapter had found themselves in such a situation—accepting the spectre of boys' disadvantage in early childhood education, cognisant that female teachers are likely complicit in this, and desiring different ways to connect with and address boys' special characteristics. Yet, if they had stopped to consider the actual tamariki they worked with and the ways these children engaged with curriculum in early childhood education, would they have identified any of them as disadvantaged in their respective early childhood contexts? Maybe—but maybe not: the key actions would be those of actually *looking*, of resisting their capture in dominant discourses, and of determining which boys, if any, were not engaging with the curriculum and why.

Teaching at this sociohistorical/sociopolitical juncture, where the boy turn has gained momentum and in which boys' and men's disadvantage has been and is being constructed so convincingly in Aotearoa New Zealand education, it is easy to see how one may become complicit in dominant discourses of boys' underachievement and the feminised workforce in early childhood education. But what does this mean for teaching towards inclusion? And how does it sit with the curriculum as we practise it within our respective early childhood settings when the expectations within *Te Whāriki* (Ministry of Education, 1996) are for kaiako to engage with tamariki in ways mindful of the issues of fairness, difference and equity?

I argue that, rather than working for gender diversity and, therefore, towards inclusion, discourses such as the ones emphasised in this chapter reinforce gender essentialism. They work to re-inscribe traditional and narrow conceptualisations of what it means to be legitimately male and female. They invoke the gender binary and seek to fix gender to a narrow frame. In such a climate, opportunities for boys, men, girls and women to learn about and express their genders in complex and diverse ways are constrained because the discourses tend to hold them to frameworks that construct them in a particular manner and as *naturally at odds* with one another. Critically engaging with gender diversity and discourse analysis may be one way to help us move beyond this point.

Discourse analysis is a powerful tool for examining how teachers approach gender (MacNaughton, 1998). Once we recognise that individuals are not simply passive recipients of imposed social structures, we have a measure of clarity that allows us to analyse practices, events or texts that we find troubling in order to move with or beyond them. If, for instance, we see a child chastise another for not being "properly" feminine or masculine, we can intervene. By drawing children's attention to the legitimacy of difference, we may help them explore what it means to not expect everyone to be *the same kind* of boy or girl.

Such disruptions to the misappropriation of power can provide conditions for equity, gender diversity and inclusion to prevail. Discourse analysis can furthermore help us to think more systematically about dominant beliefs, so-called necessary practices, and our emotional investments in them (Gunn & Surtees, 2004). Kaiako such as those referred to in this chapter's opening quote might learn a great deal through such analysis—and find that the knowledge gained can result in successful resistance to the ideas we contest and to further engagement with those we support. Like others (e.g., Cushman, 2011; Younger & Warrington, 2008), I consider that initial and ongoing teacher education has a significant role to play here.

Conclusions

Inclusion, in the context of this volume, is about recognising, understanding and addressing barriers to participation. I consider that recently deployed and prominent gender discourses about boys' underachievement and the feminised workforce within education in Aotearoa New Zealand have not worked towards this aim. Rather, they have constructed barriers. This is because these discourses draw on traditional and essentialising concepts that frame education within schools and early childhood education settings as a problem for boys and men, and that attempt to shape them and women and girls into inequitable patterns of relations.

I therefore maintain that all kaiako, not just those of us in early childhood education, must put gender back on the table and examine more closely the ways in which gender discourses are being deployed through everyday practices and assumptions in educational settings. Do those of us working within the early childhood field, where the lack of male teachers has heightened the use and embellishment of such discourses, really want to perpetuate them once we realise that they limit understanding and diverse constructions of gender? Can we instead critically engage with those ideas and show them for the constructions they are and, from there, advocate for something fairer and more inclusive? Engaging with discourse analysis is one means of disrupting the status quo. Resisting gender essentialism and working with gender diversity can facilitate inclusion. If we accept this premise, the question then becomes one of how we might best continue this work. Or, for some of us, when might we begin?

References

Alsop, R., Fitzsimons, A., & Lennon, K. (2002). *Theorizing gender*. Malden, MA: Blackwell.

Barker, B. (1997). Girls' world or anxious times? What's really happening at school in the gender war? *Educational Review, 49*(3), 221–227.

Burman, E. (2005). Childhood, neo-liberalism and the feminization of education. *Gender and Education, 17*(4), 351–367.

Burr, V. (1995). *An introduction to social constructionism*. London, UK: Routledge.

Cushman, P. (2011). "You're not a teacher, you're a man": The need for a greater focus on gender studies in teacher education. *International Journal of Inclusive Education*. doi:10.1080/13603116.2010.516774

Davies, B. (1989a). *Frogs and snails and feminist tales: Preschool children and gender*. Brisbane, QLD: Allen & Unwin.

Davies, B. (1989b). The discursive production of the male/female dualism in school settings. *Oxford Review of Education, 15*(3), 229–241.

Davies, B. (1994). *Poststructuralist theory and classroom practice*. Geelong, VIC: Deakin University Press.

Derrida, J. (1976). *Of grammatology* (G. C. Spivak, trans.). Baltimore, MD: Johns Hopkins Press.

Derrida, J. (1978). The retrait of metaphor. *Enclitic, 2*, 5–33.

ERO (Education Review Office). (1999). *The achievement of boys*. Wellington: Author.

ERO (Education Review Office). (2008). *Boys' education: Good practice in secondary schools*. Wellington: Author.

Farquhar, S., Cablk, L., Buckingham, A., Butler, D., & Ballantyne, R. (2006). *Men at work: Sexism in early childhood education*. Porirua: Childforum Research Network.

Foucault, M. (1969). *The archaeology of knowledge* (A. M. Sheridan Smith, trans.). London, UK: Routledge.

Foucault, M. (1977). *Power/knowledge: Selected interviews and other writings 1972–1977* (C. Fordon, L. Marshall, J. Mepham, & K. Soper, trans.). New York, NY: Pantheon Books.

Gergen, K. (1999). *An invitation to social construction.* London, UK: Sage Publications.

Gunn, A., & Surtees, N. (2004). Engaging with dominance and knowing our desires: New possibilities for addressing sexualities matters in early childhood education. *Journal of the New Zealand Educational Administration and Leadership Society. Special Issue: Social Justice, 19,* 79–91.

Gunn, A. C., & MacNaughton, G. (2007). Boys and boyhoods: The problems and possibilities of equity and gender diversity. In L. Keesing-Styles & H. Hedges (Eds.), *Theorising early childhood practice: Emerging dialogues* (pp. 121–136). Castle Hill, NSW: Pademelon Press.

Halliday, J., & McNaughton, S. (1982). Sex differences in play at kindergarten. *New Zealand Journal of Educational Studies, 17*(2), 161–170.

Lashlie, C. (2004). *"It's about boys": The Good Man Project.* Nelson: Nelson College for Boys.

MacNaughton, G. (1998). Improving our gender equity "tools": A case for discourse analysis. In N. Yelland (Ed.), *Gender in early childhood* (pp. 149–174). London, UK: Routledge.

MacNaughton, G. (2000). *Rethinking gender in early childhood education.* St Leonards, NSW: Allen & Unwin.

Mallard, T. (2004, 29 March). *Investigation into boys' achievement at secondary.* [New Zealand Government press release].

Martino, W. (2008). Male teachers as role models: Addressing issues of masculinity, pedagogy and the re-masculinization of schooling. *Curriculum Inquiry, 38*(2), 189–223.

McMillan, B. (1978). The role of pre-schools in the development of sex roles. In B. O'Rourke & J. Clough (Eds.), *Early childhood in New Zealand: Proceedings of the first New Zealand Early Childhood Care and Development Convention* (pp. 114–120). Auckland: Heinemann Educational Books.

Meade, A., & Staden, F. (1985). *Once upon a time, amongst the blocks and car cases.* Wellington: New Zealand Council for Educational Research.

Ministry of Education. (1996). *Te whāriki: He whāriki mātauranga mō ngā mokopuna o Aotearoa: Early childhood curriculum.* Wellington: Learning Media.

Ministry of Education. (2011). *Success for boys* [website]. Wellington: Author. Retrieved from http://success-for- boys.tki.org.nz/

Ministry of Women's Affairs, (2011). *Pānui October – Whiringa-ā-Nuku 2011.* Wellington: Author.

Skinner, J. (2006, 24 September). Men in early childhood education. *Sunday* [television current affairs programme]. Auckland: Television New Zealand.

Smith, A. B. (1985). Teacher modelling and sex-typed play preferences. *New Zealand Journal of Educational Studies, 20*(1), 39–47.

Smith, N. (2003). *Schools of excellence: Discussion paper by Dr Nick Smith, National Party education spokesperson.* Wellington: New Zealand National Party. Retrieved from http://www.national.org.nz/files/Schools_of_excellence. pdf

Titus, J. J. (2004). Boy trouble: Rhetorical framing of boys' underachievement. *Discourse: Studies in the Cultural Politics of Education, 25*(2), 145–169.

Walkerdine, V. (1981). Sex, power and pedagogy. *Screen Education, 38,* 14–23.

Weaver-Hightower, M. (2003). The "boy turn" in research on gender and education. *Review of Educational Research, 73*(4), 471–498.

Weedon, C. (1987). *Feminist practice and poststructuralist theory.* Oxford, UK: Blackwell Publishers.

Younger, M., & Warrington, M. (2008). The gender agenda in primary teacher education in England: Fifteen lost years? *Journal of Education Policy, 23*(4), 429–445.

CHAPTER 8

Does God go to preschool?: A case for religious inclusion

Bradley Hannigan

Ironically, the title of this chapter is exclusionary, as not all religions include God as the focus of worship. However here the intention is to be provocative rather than normative: to provoke further thinking rather than to define exactly what must be done and how. This chapter aims to problematise the absence of religion in secular early childhood settings. It assumes that culture has religious aspects and that, for some cultures, religion cannot be separated from cultural experience. The drive towards cultural inclusion exemplified by the early childhood curriculum *Te Whāriki* (Ministry of Education, 1996) is a fine one. This chapter builds on that direction by arguing for the inclusion of diverse religious cultures and religious aspects of culture in secular early childhood settings in Aotearoa New Zealand.

The first part of this chapter advances the argument that the exclusion of religion in secular early childhood education has discursive components (Foucault, 1972). My aim is to highlight possible reasons for the disappearance of religious discourse from education in general, and from early childhood education in particular. The second part of this chapter advances the argument that the inclusion of religious cultures (cultures for whom religion is no different to cultural experience) and religious aspects of culture (cultures for whom religion is a significant component of cultural experience) relates to a broader concern for social tolerance and cultural inclusion. Statistical evidence is used to highlight the scale of religious identity in Aotearoa New Zealand, and justifications are put forward for pursuing religious inclusion in secular early childhood settings. The third part of this chapter offers practical suggestions for how inclusion with respect to religion might be achieved.

PART ONE: The disappearance of religion

French philosopher Michel Foucault (1926–1984) wrote, among many other things, about the power of discourse to construct understanding and, subsequently, practice. To Foucault (1972, p. 49), discourses are the "practices that systematically form the objects of which they speak." From this perspective, discourse is less concerned with knowledge as an object and more concerned both with the rules by which knowledge is constructed and with the techniques by which power relationships present in the act of knowledge construction are obscured from view. For Foucault (1972, p. 27), an analysis of discourse entails asking the question, "How is it that one particular statement appeared rather than another?" Foucault wondered what it takes to make one way of describing/inscribing the world appear *normal*, and how the same discursive process simultaneously describes/inscribes *abnormality*. This chapter uses the terms *normal* and *abnormal* to highlight the difference between *familiar* and *strange*. The disappearance being pointed out here is the *abnormality* of religion-based discourse in contemporary secular early childhood settings.

Religious affiliation has not disappeared altogether in Aotearoa New Zealand. In the 2006 Census, 2,241,540 New Zealanders claimed religious affiliation (Statistics New Zealand, 2007). However, when religious affiliation is viewed as a time trend, between 1996 and 2006 the number fell by over 40,000, even though the population of the country grew by nearly 400,000 over this time (Statistics New Zealand, 2007). One number that is on the increase, however, is the number of respondents claiming no religious affiliation. In 1996 this group numbered 867,264; in 2006 it numbered 1,297,104 (Statistics New Zealand, 2007). In light of this trend, the disappearance proposed in this chapter can be seen to have a much longer history. It is related to the disappearance of religion from *public* discourse and, more specifically, the disappearance of religion from *educational* discourse in Aotearoa New Zealand.

The central claim of this part of the chapter is that secular cultural discourse has displaced the topic of religion from education—has caused its disappearance. Put another way, the normalisation of secular discourse has made religious discourse appear abnormal in educational settings. The word "secular" comes from the Latin *saecularis*, meaning *belonging to the world*. With this meaning in mind, Benson (2000) defines secularism according to its adherents' disbelief in metaphysics (otherworldliness) and a compulsion to naturalise human effort, rather than meaning simply *anti-religious*. Secularism is also synonymous with the separation of state and religion (Rawls, 1993), with religion being relegated to the realm of the private, and state business, such as education, remaining firmly within the public realm. The privatisation of religion is, in part, a product of life in democracies such as Aotearoa New Zealand that have institutionalised the Rawlsian slogan "Take the truths of religion off the political agenda" (Rawls, 1993, p. 151), and, as I argue in this chapter, off the educational agenda.

Prior to 1877, much of the education available to young tamariki in Aotearoa New Zealand had a strong religious component, due in large part to the missionaries who taught in schools throughout the country (May, 1997). In 1877 the New Zealand Education Act came into force, creating a vision for compulsory education in Aotearoa New Zealand which has survived to this day: teaching in primary schools should be "entirely of a secular character" (New Zealand Education Act 1989, s.77b). According to Adhar (2006), the shift to a secular system of education was "an attempt to diffuse sectarian strife" (p. 618).

Regardless of the origins, historians such as Adhar (2006) and Michael King (2003) agree that the path traversed during the 20th century was one of increasing secularisation in Aotearoa New Zealand—a trend that has continued into the 21st century, although the 1964 Education Act allows space for both religious instruction and observance in schools. In my whānau, my parents recall daily compulsory religious observance as part of their experiences of state schooling during the 1950s in Aotearoa New Zealand. I recall fragmented attention to religion in my early education in the late 1970s. But my children's education is almost entirely devoid of reference to religion and religious discourse. Early childhood education, in my view, has generally followed a similar trajectory, with many of today's kaiako viewing the separation of religion and education unproblematically or, rather, simply as *the order of things.* This, in itself, is an example of the normalisation of secular discourse in education: remember that secular teaching is not legislated in early childhood education as it is in the primary sector.

This is not to say that religion and early childhood education are mutually exclusive. Currently there are 67 schools in the New Zealand Association for Christian Schools and 72 early childhood services in the Christian Early Childhood Education Association of Aotearoa. These figures do not include other early childhood centres that integrate Christian beliefs and education but which do not belong to either association. Bethlehem Tertiary Institute offers teacher education courses at early childhood, primary and secondary levels that integrate pedagogy with a Christian world view. There are currently two Muslim and state-integrated schools in the country (both in Auckland), one Islamic early childhood centre in Canterbury, and two Jewish schools in Aotearoa New Zealand, along with two early childhood centres. At present there are no Buddhist schools or early childhood services. Thus, there are instances where education and religion co-exist. That said, in 2010 there were 4,321 licensed early childhood services in Aotearoa New Zealand (Castillo, 2010). Given the small number of early childhood services with a religious affiliation, it is justifiable to say that many, if not most, early childhood services in this country have a secular affiliation.

With secularism prevalent in the discursive context, it is easy to understand how alternative discourses, which are made silent through social and cultural reproduction, have no place in our collective experience of education. Secular notions of education and its uses, particularly insofar as they are confirmed in our experience of education, and our experience of contemporary early childhood settings, appear *normal*. Other discourses, such as those that use religious terminology are, because they contradict the normal order of things, either marked as *abnormal* or repressed altogether; that is, until such time as a child's diet or a family's religious conviction (e.g., observing halal requirements or not celebrating birthdays) calls the secular discourse into question. Within highly secularised settings, religious convictions seem perverse, foreign, abnormal— not because they are, but because convictions based on religious discourse are abnormal within a discursive field dominated by secular assumption.

The disappearance of religion at the level of educational discourse in secular early childhood settings takes the form of an eclipsing—an overtaking, an exclusion. This is particularly relevant to those contexts in which secular discourses have phrased religion not only as a private concern but also as publically obsolete. Within this frame, religion is a part of the self that is best kept hidden from view—a part of the self that does not belong; a contribution that requires no public expression, let alone any possibility for fruitful exploration. For those among the 1,297,104 who claim no religion, this does not look like a problem at all; it is business as usual. But for the 2,241,540 who claim religious affiliation, calls to integrate home life into the life of the centre (Ministry of Education, 1996) come with a proviso: it is the secular body—the body with the religious organs cut off—that is invited.

PART TWO: A case for religious inclusion

Contemporary early childhood education in Aotearoa New Zealand adopts a focus on cultural inclusion that permeates curriculum (Ministry of Education, 1996), assessment (Ministry of Education, 2004/09), policy (Ministry of Education, 2002) and vision. For example, the early childhood curriculum *Te Whāriki* (Ministry of Education, 1996) directs kaiako to "promote and protect" (p. 16) language and symbols of their own and other cultures, to "help children gain a positive awareness of their own and other cultures" (p. 18), to respect cultural knowledge (p. 42), to acknowledge different cultures (p. 55), and to "encompass different cultural perspectives, recognising and affirming the primary importance of the child's family and culture" (p. 65). These commitments are not, of course, surprising given the sociocultural assumptions (Te One, 2003) that underpin the content and aspirations of *Te Whāriki* and early childhood education in Aotearoa New Zealand (Ministry of Education, 1996).

The key theorists who inform early childhood education in Aotearoa New Zealand highlight the importance of cultural context in terms of human development, cognition and pedagogy. For example, according to Vygotsky (1978), "every function in the child's cultural development appears twice: first, on the social level, and later, on the individual level" (p. 57). Vygotsky called the mechanism for this process *internalisation*. He believed that tamariki (and humans in general) are socially and historically situated beings. For Vygotsky (1978, p. 56), this approach meant that learning, even that acquired from the earliest experiences, is not purely object directed; rather, it is directed by the reactions of others and interactions with others in the person's social context. Writing within this line of reasoning, Rogoff (1990) later observed that "it is essential to view the cognitive activities of individuals within the cultural context in which their thinking is embedded" (p. 42). Vygotsky and Rogoff have had a strong influence on contemporary discourses of early childhood education. They each take cultural inclusion as a central motif in their writing on learning and education. And both, along with Bronfenbrenner (1979)—incidentally the only theorist openly cited in *Te Whāriki*—highlight the profound importance of culture on learning, identity and belonging.

My aim here is not to challenge the dominance of discourses of cultural inclusion, but rather to challenge the normality of a purely secular understanding of culture. Although not everybody would like their religious beliefs included in the culture of an early childhood setting, this is no reason to continue with the exclusion of cultural discourses that include religion and religious commitments. It may be that families do not wish to appear *abnormal* in secular normalised early childhood settings. However, as discourses shift from solely secular to religion inclusive so, too, does the distinction between normal and abnormal. It is reasonable, then, to expect that the more normal religious cultures look and the more normal religious aspects of culture appear, the more likely it is that whānau will express those aspects of their collective self within the wider community. Secularism is not eroded as a result, but rather expanded to include incommensurable discourses. I shall call this a mature secularism, as opposed to naive secularism, which reacts against incommensurable discourses by entrenching its own.

Aside from expanding the discourse on cultural inclusion to encompass religion, there is the children's rights argument in support of religious discourse in education. The United Nations Convention on the Rights of the Child states that "every child and young person has the right to freedom of thought, conscience and religion (unless there are legal restrictions)" (United Nations, 1989, article 14). Given the lack of legal restriction in early childhood education, it is conceivable that the disappearance of religious discourse within centres—the absence of vocabulary and symbol and the avoidance of religious imagery—curtails the possibility of a child's freedom of religion within these contexts. Why should this be? One answer is that people (tamariki included) learn within common spaces that shape not only possible meanings but also possible identities (Wenger, 1998). In spaces that exclude religion (such as secular early childhood settings), possibilities for meaning making and identity formation are restricted. This situation, in turn, reproduces the normalisation of secular discourse and, subsequently, the privatisation of religion. In this way, the right to freedom of religion appears abnormal and, as such, is subverted through a subtle enculturation.

There is a small but interesting body of literature emerging on the role of religion in building relationships within families, and between families and educational settings, a subject closely connected to the principles of *Te Whāriki*. Studies on the effect of religion on parent–child bonding show that religion enhances the development of strong, positive relationships (V. King, 2003; Wilcox, 2002). Other research suggests that religion also acts to sanctify the family unit (Mahoney, Pargament, Murray-Swank, & Murray-Swank, 2003), providing a narrative that binds whānau members together in their common belief. Smith (2003) found that non-parental relationships which reinforce parental values result in greater prosocial outcomes for older tamariki, particularly in terms of community connectedness. Sympathetic to findings such as these, Stower and Ryan (1998) propose that "religious experience contributes to the development of the whole child and should be respected, encouraged, and supported by caregivers and teachers" (p. 1). This research is important in a context that assumes the forging of strong links between home-life and centre-life is important if tamariki are to develop a positive awareness of their own culture, as well as a positive awareness of their own identity in relation to others.

Literature on religion from the field of multicultural education supports the notion that acknowledging religious aspects of children's culture encourages social tolerance (Jones, 2010) and intercultural understanding (Han & Thomas, 2010), while simultaneously promoting a broadly inclusive environment (Ang, 2010). The above writers agree that religion is an important facet in the cultural make-up of many children's lives. When religion is absent from early childhood settings, an important part of the culture of tamariki and their whānau is edited out. On this point, Crompton (1999) writes, "attention to an understanding of children's religious backgrounds, beliefs, and observances is an essential means of demonstration of respect for, and interest in, every aspect of their lives" (p. 84), not just those aspects that appear normal within secular settings. Religious inclusion is therefore a necessary component of cultural inclusion. It enables the inclusion of diverse families into the life of the centre (Couchenour & Chrisman, 2003). In so doing, it encourages tamariki to "gain a positive awareness of their own and other cultures" (Ministry of Education, 1996, p. 18).

Linked to the ethic of cultural inclusion, concern for holistic development and holistic wellbeing is embedded within *Te Whāriki*. The concept of spiritual wellbeing, or taha wairua, within the articulation of holistic development used in *Te Whāriki*, is particularly relevant to the subject of religious inclusion in early childhood education. There is a growing body of literature concerned with spirituality in secular early childhood settings (e.g., Bone, 2005, 2008, 2009; Pedraza, 2006; Upton, 2009). This interest in spirituality resonates with the aspiration in the curriculum that tamariki grow up "healthy in mind, body and spirit" (Ministry of Education, 1996, p. 9); and particularly with the assertion that holistic learning and development is enhanced through "the recognition of the spiritual dimension of children's lives in culturally, socially, and individually appropriate ways" (Ministry of Education, 1996, p. 41). The notion of spiritual development is important here because religion and spirituality are not necessarily mutually exclusive. However, it must be added that the word "religion" does not appear at all in *Te Whāriki*—but then neither does the word "happy".

There are, of course, differences between religion and spirituality. Mehler (2005), for example, describes spirituality as an experiential realisation and religion as a social organisation; as "the business that has evolved out of spirituality" (p. 14). Vaughan (1991) similarly links religion to institutionalised belief and spirituality to "a subjective experience of the sacred" (p. 105). But there are also powerful similarities. For example, the Education Forum (1998), in their submission regarding spirituality in the Aotearoa New Zealand health curriculum, noted that religion has spiritual dimensions in much the same way as spirituality has religious dimensions. Miller and Thoresen (2003) run "religion" and "spirituality" together, using them interchangeably to mean the same thing, while Moberg (2005) proposes that religion and spirituality intersect to such a degree that it makes little sense to speak of the one without entertaining consideration of the other. This idea is supported by Crompton (1999), who claims that "for many children and their families, spirituality is inseparable from religious faith" (p. 84).

Another powerful challenge to secular discourse comes from te ao Māori in the context of the bicultural aspirations outlined in and exemplified by *Te Whāriki*. According to Durie (1994), Hemara (2000) and Pere (1997), spirituality is a necessary part of Māori culture. Within this frame, separating spiritual (and subsequently religious) aspects of self and culture from education and educational settings contradicts the bicultural aspirations of *Te Whāriki*. I would argue, therefore, that a commitment to biculturalism provides further justification for religious inclusion, and even more so when we consider findings from the 2006 Census. Of the 565,300 people who identified themselves as Māori, 245,052 also identified themselves as Christian, 10,775 as Buddhist, 1,074 as Muslim and 816 as Hindu (Statistics New Zealand, 2007). With this diversity of spiritual and religious belief within te ao Māori coupled with a commitment to biculturalism, a one-size-fits-all approach to cultural inclusion will not suffice. What is required is a far broader approach whereby diversity can flourish on its own terms.

This chapter argues that the current of cultural inclusion that has run through early childhood education in Aotearoa New Zealand, particularly since the early 1980s (May, 2009), paves the way for religious inclusion in early childhood education. The will to forge stronger links between home and centre experiences (e.g., Ministry of Education, 1996, 2002) supports this expansion, as does the notion of the *whole child* and the literature on the role of religion in holistic wellbeing (e.g., Haight, 2001). For those tamariki who come from cultures where religion and culture mean the same thing (as in some forms of Islam, Hinduism, Buddhism and Christianity), it is not possible, as indicated earlier, to exclude religion from culture; to do so would be a contradiction in terms. This last point is particularly important given that the population of minority religious cultures is on the increase in Aotearoa New Zealand. For example, between the 1996 and 2006 censuses, the number of people in Aotearoa New Zealand identifying as Muslim increased from 13,545 to 36,072 (Statistics New Zealand, 2007). The number of people identifying as Hindu and Buddhist also increased over the same period (from 25,551 to 64,392 and from 28,131 to 52,362, respectively). A similar trend can be observed over the same period in the specifically Māori religions of Ratana (with 36,450 people reporting this religious affiliation in 1996 and 50,565 in 2006) and Ringatū (8,271 people in 1996 and 16,419 in 2006) (Statistics New Zealand, 2007).

When these numbers are considered in relation to the total population of Aotearoa New Zealand (just over 4 million at the time of the 2006 Census), they are not huge, but their increase raises the possibility of tamariki and their whānau from these cultures enrolling in early childhood education. Add to that the 2,027,000 people who identified as Christian at the time of the 2006 Census, and it is clear that a great number of tamariki and their families have religious aspects to their culture. If we are serious about cultural inclusion, then religious cultures and religious aspects of culture must also be included. This is not to say that everyone wants the walls painted with their religious beliefs, but rather that religious diversity, education and social tolerance are intricately linked (Amor, 2001).

PART THREE: Suggestions for encouraging religious inclusion

The first part of this chapter discussed a general problem that has serious repercussions for anyone interested in religious inclusion in early childhood education in Aotearoa New Zealand; namely, the disappearance of religious discourse in secular education settings. This disappearance creates a barrier in the form of a general culturally reproduced ignorance. What I mean by this is that most kaiako in Aotearoa New Zealand who were educated in state primary and secondary schools have had very little formal education relating to religious diversity outside of the occasional social studies project. The secular character of schooling in Aotearoa New Zealand and the lack of a religious education curriculum have meant that entire vocabularies pertaining to religion, as well as the ideas surrounding those vocabularies, have been edited out of public discourse. Over time, this cultural ignoring of religion in secular society has bred a group of people who have lost the ability to hold conversations about cultures that include religion or religious perspectives, or a combination of both. I consider this to be a great pity.

The same cannot be said about the United Kingdom. There, the 1988 Education Reform Act (s.8) made religious education a compulsory part of the state school curriculum. The inclusion of religion in the official educational agenda meant that all students of school age were given access to religious vocabulary, religious themes and religious aspects of culture across a wide variety of religious expressions (McKenna, Neill, & Jackson, 2009). In their study of the effect of religious education on tolerance in England, McKenna et al. (2009) found that affirming faith aspects of culture and learning about diverse faiths resulted in a greater degree of social tolerance coupled with an inclination to enter into dialogue regarding issues of religion. Arguably, the absence of religious education reduces not only the opportunity for dialogue but also one's ability to tolerate diverse religious world views (Knauth, 2011). Educating kaiako is therefore a key challenge in regard to the support of religious inclusion.

One powerful method for normalising religion in secular early childhood settings is to include the study of religious diversity in initial teacher education programmes, and in professional development programmes for qualified kaiako. This is the same sort of reasoning that advocates for inclusion have used to great effect (e.g., Purdue, Gordon-Burns, Gunn, Madden, & Surtees, 2009). In relation to religious inclusion, Brown, Wiggins and Secord (2008) identify teacher education programmes as sites where personal ideas about religion and religions can be questioned, challenged and, if necessary, changed with a view towards social tolerance and inclusion. The point here is that without education about religious diversity, kaiako will not have the resources (i.e., the vocabulary and conceptual framework) with which to even begin to think about what religious inclusion might look like as an idea, let alone what it might look like in practice.

One potential barrier that religious inclusion might encounter is the construction of a microcosm for religious conflict. For example, in Islam, depictions of Allah and/or the Prophet Muhammad are forbidden in the *hadith* (or sayings) of the Prophet Muhammad. However, in Hinduism, depictions of the personalities of the Godhead are encouraged as mediums for both prayer and devotion in the act of *darshan* (or being seen by the deity). Similarly Judeo/Christian/Islamic/Hindu religious traditions are premised on the belief in an eternal soul, whereas Buddhism is premised on the absence of a permanent soul. These tensions have translated into much conflict and even bloodshed throughout human history. The prospect of offending can be daunting from the outset, and may dissuade even the most earnest efforts at religious inclusion. However, this need not be the case. Consultation with people from diverse religious communities will not only allay such fears but will also reflect a strong commitment to forging bonds with members of the wider community within which the early childhood centre is embedded (in both a physical and a social sense).

A second—and perhaps more pertinent—barrier to religious inclusion in early childhood settings in Aotearoa New Zealand relates to the pragmatics of what can actually be done. This chapter concludes with some suggestions on religion-inclusive practices in the hope that you, the reader, might take up the challenge of implementing and building on these suggestions in your practice. The list of ideas is by no means exhaustive; it is only a beginning, a tentative sketch of what has worked in early childhood settings.

According to Zeece (1998), children's literature is a useful medium for introducing tamariki to diverse religions. Zeece proposes that literature that introduces tamariki to "other religions encourages youngsters to understand and respect religion-based differences" (p. 245). The principle here is similar to that employed by those who challenge heteronormativity by including literature (resources) portraying same-sex parents in centres and in kaiako education programmes (see, for example, Herman-Wilmarth, 2010). Literature in these contexts has multiple uses. First, it gives tamariki access to ideas usually subverted in secular society (religion); second, it allows tamariki to develop curiosity and interest in diverse others and their beliefs; and third, it normalises religion and multiple religions through recognition that religious difference exists as part of the world that tamariki live in. Finally, for those who belong to religious cultures or whose own culture has religious aspects, the inclusion of religion-based literature affirms that their identity is recognised and valued within the culture of the centre. Books such as *Many Ways: How Families Practice Their Beliefs and Religions* (Rotner & Kelly, 2006) and *A Faith Like Mine: A Celebration of the World's Religions Through the Eyes of Children* (Buller, 2005) are good examples of useful literature for religious inclusion.

Another way of creating religion-inclusive settings for young tamariki is through the celebration of diverse religious festivals such as Matariki, Diwali, Easter, Baisakhi, Purim, Solstice and Eid-ul-fitr, to name but a few. Encouraging the celebration of diverse religious festivals offers tamariki the opportunity to experience the art, crafts, food, stories and languages of diverse cultures. Including multi-faith celebrations in the centre calendar normalises diversity and can generate positive experiences and perceptions of difference. *Festivals Together: A Guide to Multi-Cultural Celebration* (Fitzjohn, Weston, & Large, 1999) is an excellent resource in this regard.

This suggestion may be criticised as a *tourist* approach to multiculturalism. For those of us dealing with young tamariki in a largely secular society, I think this approach is unavoidable. In-depth study of religious belief is clearly not appropriate in these settings. I am suggesting here that the experience of celebration may encourage social tolerance of diversity in a practical sense of doing, tasting and vocalising. However, I am not proposing that this suggestion alone is enough to be considered religious inclusion. A further way that religious inclusion can be put into action is through identifying places, spaces and symbols that are important to different religions (Dalley, 2010), such as the Ka'bah and the crescent in Islam, the Church of the Holy Sepulchre and the cross in Christianity, and Bodh Gaya and the lotus flower in Buddhism.

These various ways of encouraging religious inclusion contain the possibility of sparking conversations and explorations relating to subjects such as food, art, music, buildings and countries throughout the world. As tamariki learn more about religious cultures, they are likely to become more socially tolerant and less fearful of diversity (Dalley, 2010). For those tamariki whose religious culture or religious aspects of their culture are included within the culture of the centre, the benefits are most likely to be an enhanced sense of identity, belonging and community. These benefits are all actively encouraged in *Te Whāriki* and in early childhood settings throughout Aotearoa New Zealand.

Conclusion

Teaching practice based on an ethic of cultural inclusion provides a powerful tool for the construction of a socially tolerant, inclusive society. This chapter has argued that secular constructions of culture make religious cultural expressions appear abnormal, especially within secular early childhood settings. A number of justifications have been put forward to support a case for religious inclusion in such settings in the hope that readers are provoked to question their own assumptions on inclusion, as well as culturally inherited assumptions on religion in secular settings. Some suggestions have been made on what religious inclusion might look like, but these are meant as mere starting points. The real challenge lies in how these ideas can be put into practice to make a difference in the lives of tamariki and their whānau.

References

Adhar, R. (2006). Reflections on the path of religion–state relations in New Zealand. *Brigham Young University Law Review*, 3, 619–660.

Amor, A. (2001, November). *The role of religious education in the pursuit of tolerance and non-discrimination*. Paper presented at the International Consultative Conference on School Education in Relation with Freedom of Religion and Belief, Tolerance and Non-Discrimination, Madrid, Spain.

Ang, L. (2010). Critical perspectives on cultural diversity in early childhood: Building an inclusive curriculum and provision. *Early Years*, 30(1), 41–52.

Benson, I. (2000). Notes toward a (re)definition of the secular. *University of British Columbia Law Review*, 33(3), 519–550.

Bone, J. (2005). Breaking bread: Spirituality, food and early childhood education. *International Journal of Children's Spirituality*, 10(3), 307–317.

Bone, J. (2008). Creating relational spaces: Everyday spirituality in early childhood settings. *European Early Childhood Education Research Journal*, 16(3), 343–356.

Bone, J. (2009). Narratives of everyday spirituality: Pedagogical perspectives from three early childhood settings in Aotearoa New Zealand. In M. De Souza, L. Francis, J. O'Higgins-Norman, & D. Scott (Eds.), *International handbook of education for spirituality* (pp. 873–890). New York, NY: Springer.

Bronfenbrenner, U. (1979). *The ecology of human development: Experiments by nature and design*. Cambridge, MA: Harvard University Press.

Brown, N., Wiggins, R., & Secord, D. (2008). "And God sits next to me": The role of religion in teacher education programs. In M. Heston, D. Tidwell, K. East, & L. Fitzgerald (Eds.), *The Seventh International Conference on Self-Study of Teacher Education Practices: Pathways to change in teacher education: Dialogue, diversity and self-study*. Cedar Falls, IA: University of Northern Iowa.

Buller, L. (2005). *A faith like mine: A celebration of the world's religions through the eyes of children*. London, UK: Dorling Kindersley.

Castillo, E. (2010). *Number of licensed early childhood services*. Wellington: Ministry of Education.

Couchenour, D., & Chrisman, K. (2003). *Families, schools, and communities: Together for young children*. Clifton Park, NY: Thomson Delmar Learning.

Crompton, M. (1999). Children, spirituality, and religion. In P. Milner & B. Carolin (Eds.), *Time to listen to children: Personal and professional communication* (pp. 79–96). London, UK: Routledge.

Dalley, D. (2010). *Honouring the religious and spiritual identities of children in early childhood education: A workshop by the Surrey Neighbouring Faiths Program.* Surrey, British Columbia, Canada: Surrey Neighbouring Faiths Program.

Durie, M. (1994). *Whaiora: Māori health development.* Auckland: Oxford University Press.

Education Forum. (1998). *Health and physical education in the New Zealand curriculum: A submission on the draft.* Wellington: Author.

Fitzjohn, S., Weston, M., & Large, J. (1999). *Festivals together: A guide to multicultural celebration.* Stroud, UK: Hawthorn Press.

Foucault, M. (1972). *The archaeology of knowledge and the discourse on language.* New York, NY: Pantheon Books.

Haight, W. L. (2001). *African American children at church: A sociological study.* New York, NY: Teachers College Press.

Han, H. S., & Thomas, M. S. (2010). No child misunderstood: Enhancing early childhood teachers' multicultural responsiveness to the social competence of diverse children. *Early Childhood Education Journal, 37*(6), 469–476.

Hemara, W. (2000). *Māori pedagogies: A review from the literature.* Wellington: New Zealand Council for Educational Research.

Herman-Wilmarth, J. (2010). More than book talks: Preservice teacher dialogue after reading gay and lesbian children's literature. *Language Arts, 87*(3), 188–198.

Jones, P. N. (2010). Toleration and recognition: What should we teach? In M. Sardoč (Ed.), *Toleration, respect and recognition in education* (pp. 33–51). Oxford, UK: Wiley- Blackwell.

King, M. (2003). *The Penguin history of New Zealand.* Auckland: Penguin Books.

King, V. (2003). The influence of religion on fathers' relationships with their children. *Journal of Marriage and Family, 65,* 382–395.

Knauth, T. (2011). Tolerance: A key concept for dealing with cultural and religious diversity in education. In F. Tibbitts, R. Jackson, D. Kerr, T. Knauth, & P. Kirchschläger (Eds.), *The EWC statement series* (pp. 18–21). Oslo, Norway: The European Wergeland Centre.

Mahoney, A., Pargament, K. I., Murray-Swank, A., & Murray-Swank, N. (2003). Religion and the sanctification of family relationships. *Review of Religious Research, 44,* 220–236.

May, H. (1997). *Discovery of early childhood: Mid eighteenth century Europe to twentieth century New Zealand.* Wellington: Bridget Williams Books.

May, H. (2009). *Politics in the playground: The world of early childhood in New Zealand* (2nd ed.). Dunedin: Otago University Press.

McKenna, U., Neill, S., & Jackson, R. (2009). Personal worldviews, dialogue and tolerance: Students' views on religious education in England. In P. Valk, G. Bertram-Troost, M. Friederici, & C. Béraud (Eds.), *Teenagers' perspectives on the role of religion in their lives, schools and societies: A European quantitative study* (pp. 49–70). New York, NY: Waxmann.

Mehler, S. (2005). *From light into darkness: The evolution in ancient Egypt.* Kempton, IL: Adventures Unlimited Press.

Miller, W., & Thoresen, C. (2003). Spirituality, religion and health. *American Psychologist, 58*(1), 24–35.

Ministry of Education. (1996). *Te whāriki: He whāriki mātauranga mō ngā mokopuna o Aotearoa: Early childhood curriculum.* Wellington: Learning Media.

Ministry of Education. (2002). *Pathways to the future: Ngā huarahi arataki.* Wellington: Ministry of Education.

Ministry of Education. (2004/09). *Kei tua o te pae/Assessment for learning: Early childhood exemplars.* Wellington: Learning Media.

Moberg, D. O. (2005). Research in spirituality, religion, and aging. *Journal of Gerontological Social Work, 45*(1), 11–40.

Pedraza, L. (2006). *"Because they are spiritually discerned": Spirituality in early childhood education.* Unpublished doctoral thesis, Ohio State University, Columbus, Ohio, USA.

Pere, R. (1997). *Ako: Concepts and learning in the Māori tradition.* Wellington: Te Kōhanga Reo National Trust.

Purdue, K., Gordon-Burns, D., Gunn, A., Madden, B., & Surtees, N. (2009). Supporting inclusion in early childhood settings: Some possibilities and problems for teacher education. *International Journal of Inclusive Education, 13*(8), 805–815.

Rawls, J. (1993). *Political liberalism.* New York, NY: Columbia University Press.

Rogoff, B. (1990). *Apprenticeship in thinking: Cognitive development in social context.* New York, NY: Oxford University Press.

Rotner, S., & Kelly, S. (2006). *Many ways: How families practice their beliefs and religions.* Minneapolis, MN: Millbrook Press.

Smith, C. (2003). Religious participation and network closure among American adolescents. *Journal for the Scientific Study of Religion, 42,* 259–267.

Statistics New Zealand. (2007). *Quick stats about culture and identity.* Wellington: Author.

Stower, L., & Ryan, M. (1998). A vision of the whole child: The significance of religious experiences in early childhood. *Australian Journal of Early Childhood, 23*(1), 1–4.

Te One, S. (2003). The context for *Te Whāriki*: Contemporary issues of influence. In J. Nuttall (Ed.), *Weaving Te Whāriki: Aotearoa New Zealand's early childhood curriculum document in theory and practice.* Wellington: NZCER Press.

United Nations. (1989). *The United Nations Convention on the Rights of the Child.* Geneva, Switzerland: Author.

Upton, M. (2009). Moment to moment in early childhood education. In M. De Souza, L. Francis, J. O'Higgins-Norman, & D. Scott (Eds.), *International handbook of education for spirituality* (pp. 349–363). New York, NY: Springer.

Vaughan, F. (1991). Spiritual issues in psychotherapy. *Journal of Transpersonal Psychology, 23,* 105–119.

Vygotsky, L. (1978). *Mind in society: The development of higher mental processes.* Cambridge, MA: Harvard University Press.

Wenger, E. (1998). *Communities of practice: Learning, meaning and identity.* New York, NY: Cambridge University Press.

Wilcox, W. B. (2002). Religion, convention, and paternal involvement. *Journal of Marriage and Family, 64,* 780–793.

Zeece, P. (1998). "Can God come here?" Using religion-based literature in early childhood settings. *Early Childhood Education Journal, 25*(4), 243–246.

CHAPTER 9

Key factors in creating inclusive early childhood settings for children with disabilities and their families

Diane Gordon-Burns, Kerry Purdue, Benita Rarere-Briggs,
Robyn Stark and Karen Turnock

Introduction

Inclusive education for children with disabilities and their families is premised on three key ideas:

- all children and families have the right to access and receive a quality early childhood education in their local regular early childhood service
- all children can benefit from an inclusive early childhood education
- an inclusive early childhood system is an essential component of helping create an inclusive society for all.

Inclusive education for tamariki with disabilities and their whānau is therefore about rights, social justice and equity. It involves the full participation of these children and their families, as well as of children and families from other minority groups, in all aspects of regular education settings and communities. In the Aotearoa New Zealand context, this understanding of inclusive education is premised on the notion of every child having "the right to access the culturally valued curriculum of their society and to be a full-time member of an ordinary early childhood setting or school classroom alongside other children of similar chronological age" (Ballard, 1998, p. 307).

Several developments in Aotearoa New Zealand have progressed change towards an inclusive education system faster than has occurred in many other countries. These include:

- legislation (e.g., the Education Act 1989, the Human Rights Act 1993, the Education (Early Childhood Services) Regulations 2008)
- policy and other documents supporting inclusion (e.g., Ministry of Education, 1996, 2005)
- intense advocating by parents, whānau, people with disabilities, disability organisations and inclusion supporters (Brown, 1999; Inclusive Education Action Group, 2011; Neilson, 2005)
- the implementation of the New Zealand Disability Strategy (Minister for Disability Issues, 2001)
- being a signatory to the United Nations Convention on the Rights of the Child, the United Nations Convention on the Rights of Persons with Disabilities and the UNESCO Salamanca Statement
- research highlighting the benefits of an inclusive education system for all (Fraser, Moltzen, & Ryba, 2005; Mitchell, 2008; Purdue, 2004)
- research supporting the idea that children with disabilities learn and develop best when they have access to regular education settings that are inclusive (Ballard, 2004; Macartney, 2011; Purdue, 2006).

In Aotearoa New Zealand it is against the law for any educational establishment to exclude and discriminate on the basis of disability. The New Zealand Government is committed to the goal of "changing New Zealand from a disabling to an inclusive society" (Minister for Disability Issues, 2001, p. 1). The key aim of the government's Disability Strategy is to remove the barriers to participation in society faced by people with disabilities. The strategy emphasises that working towards an inclusive and more just society must involve "improving education so that all children, youth and adult learners will have equal opportunities to learn and develop in their local, regular educational centres" (Minister for Disability Issues, 2001, p. 11).

Despite making good progress towards this reality, Aotearoa New Zealand has yet to achieve the inclusive education system and society articulated in the Disability Strategy. Exclusionary cultures, policies, pedagogies, organisational structures and resourcing continue to create barriers that limit the rights of tamariki with disabilities and their whānau to equitable education (Gordon-Burns, Purdue, Rarere-Briggs, Stark, & Turnock, 2010). It is therefore important to look at what inclusive early childhood education for children with disabilities might look like—in philosophy, policy and practice—to help teachers and others involved in the sector progress inclusion in their settings and communities.

In this chapter we highlight key factors from relevant research that, when evident in an early childhood setting, contribute to inclusive early childhood education for children with disabilities and their families. These elements should be thought of as interdependent parts in the development of truly inclusive environments for all, rather than as separate, unrelated components. We look at each of these factors in turn.

Key factors for inclusion

1. Discourses of disability

Research highlights that many discourses of disability can exist in early childhood settings. Each has different consequences (whether positive or negative) for tamariki with disabilities and their whānau (Macartney, 2011; Purdue, 2004). We briefly outline the main disability discourses—medical and special education, lay, charity, and rights. (For more information on these discourses and their effects, see Ballard, 2004; Fraser & Shields, 2010; Macartney, 2008b; Neilson, 2005.)

We ask you to reflect on the following question:

- What do the discourses you use in relation to children with disabilities tell you about your attitudes to these tamariki, and your views on teaching and including them in early childhood settings?

Do you perhaps believe that disability is an individual flaw and that "helping" children with disabilities requires fixing or treating the impairment and making them more "normal" so that they can participate more fully in society? This type of thinking about disability is, according to Skrtic (1995), very dominant in society and is influenced by medical and special education discourses of disability. These discourses locate disability within assumptions of pathology and normative differences, and see the "problems" of children with disabilities primarily as a product of their impairments. The focus, therefore, is typically on special education and other professional "experts" finding out what is wrong with the child (i.e., assessment and diagnosis) and on fixing the problem or deficit (i.e., treatment and remediation).

Within this intervention model, programmes are predominantly child-deficit focused and aim to equip the child with skills to cope with regular settings rather than adapting settings in response to the child's learning and other needs (Cullen & Carroll-Lind, 2005; Macartney, 2011; Rix, Paige-Smith, & Jones, 2008). One of the outcomes of this remedial approach is that children are labelled, perhaps even stigmatised, from an early age as negatively different and as having "special needs", a situation that favours the attitudes and practices associated with exclusion (Purdue, 2006).

Perhaps you consider children with disabilities and their families to be victims of a tragic circumstance, or maybe sources of inspiration? The charity discourse perpetuates the idea that disability is a personal tragedy. It positions tamariki with disabilities and their whānau either as objects of pity in need of protection, help and care, or as sources of inspiration because they are "coping so well" with what is assumed to be an "awful situation". As Fraser and Shields (2010) point out, the charity discourse "fails to acknowledge or identify their [people with disabilities] agency, capabilities, and capacity; hence, their voices are rarely heard and less often sought" (p. 11).

When people take a charity approach to disability, children with disabilities and their families are often subjected to hurtful comments, stares and whispers, pity and condescension, nervousness and embarrassment, ignoring and avoidance—actions all indicative of a lack of ease about and a bias towards disability. The charity discourse is also reflected in those situations where attendance and participation in early childhood education are seen as a privilege and not a right, and where decisions regarding the teaching and learning of children with disabilities can be made in the child's "best interests" by well-meaning kaiako and other professionals (Purdue, Gordon-Burns, Rarere-Briggs, Stark, & Turnock, 2011).

Maybe you feel uncomfortable about, or incapable of, including and teaching children with disabilities in early childhood settings and therefore feel these tamariki would be better off in a segregated early intervention unit? The negative assumptions and stereotypes about disability perpetuated by a lay discourse (as well as the other dominant discourses of disability) tend to exacerbate such fears and prejudices in people (Neilson, 2005). Therefore, the types of attitudes emanating from lay discourses relegate children with disabilities and their families to the position of "the other", a situation which makes them vulnerable to discrimination and exclusion.

Alternatively, do you consider *all* tamariki with disabilities to be competent and confident and as having the same rights as all other children and families to access and participate in their local, regular early childhood service? A rights and sociocultural discourse of disability promotes the view that it is disabling attitudes and environments—not the disabilities *per se*—that cause disability (Minister for Disability Issues, 2001). Such discourses also promote the view that the full inclusion and participation of children with disabilities in early childhood settings and their associated communities is the optimal strategy for ensuring that tamariki are supported to learn the knowledge, skills, dispositions and understanding relevant to their respective cultures (Ministry of Education, 1996). Kaiako who work from such models welcome all children and families into their environments, identify and eliminate barriers to learning and participation, and work to ensure that all the early childhood experiences of all tamariki and whānau are positive ones (Glass, Baker, Ellis, Bernstone, & Hagen, 2008; MacArthur, Purdue, & Ballard, 2003).

Successful inclusion in early childhood settings thus relies on discourses that promote a social justice and rights approach to disability. Early childhood teachers, managers, parents, whānau and other professionals need to continually reflect on their views, values and understandings of disability, difference and inclusion to ensure that a shared culture of inclusion resonates throughout policy and practice, and that everyone is working towards the same goal—an inclusive early childhood service and community for all (Ministry of Education, 1996; Rix, 2008).

2. Service policies

Research evidence suggests that educational settings that take a special needs approach to disability in their policies undermine any efforts they might take towards inclusiveness (Ballard, 2004; Booth,

Ainscow, & Kingston, 2006). This approach positions disability as a problem or burden for kaiako. It also positions the attendance and participation of children with disabilities as impractical, difficult to manage, time consuming and expensive. Clauses of conditionality are often evident in those parts of early childhood policies focused on tamariki with disabilities (Purdue, 2004; Slee, 1996), even though such statements can potentially breach section 57 of the Human Rights Act 1993. This focus emphasises the technical requirements needed for managing disability, such as funding, material and human resources, and training (Slee, 1996).

When such policies are applied in practice, barriers to inclusion permeate every aspect of the early childhood experiences of whānau of tamariki with disabilities because they locate the source of problems within the child and thereby absolve the service from responsibility for meeting the rights of these children. It is therefore important that teachers and management review their policies to make sure that they truly abide by the principles and values of inclusion underpinning national legislation, early childhood policies and other relevant documents (Gunn, 2003).

As a starting point, then, kaiako might ask themselves if their policies respect the legislated rights of children with disabilities and their families. If the answer is no, they then need to ask, what barriers to inclusion do we need to address to ensure they do? Government agencies responsible for monitoring and evaluating early childhood services must also make sure that early childhood settings are acting legally in policy and practice and then quickly intervene if they are not (Minister for Disability Issues, 2001).

3. Teaching practices

Research in the field of disability and inclusion recognises and accentuates the fact that teachers are key to the successful inclusion of tamariki with disabilities and their whānau within the early childhood sector (Booth et al., 2006; Corbett, 2001; Foreman, 2011). Inclusive teaching is about non-discriminatory responsive practice (MacNaughton & Williams, 2009). This can be achieved in many ways, for instance by kaiako:

- using curricular and pedagogical strategies to ensure children are supported in ways that allow them to participate, learn and develop
- willingly adapting approaches and environments as necessary
- taking responsibility for all tamariki and not relying exclusively on "specialists" and "experts" to include and teach children with disabilities
- working through issues and challenges by engaging in critical dialogue and reflection, creativity and risk-taking, co-operation and collaborative problem-solving, partnership and shared responsibility (for examples of these practices in action, see Florian, 2007).

It is therefore important that teachers are well supported and prepared to teach all tamariki, and that families of children with disabilities are not waiting for kaiako and services to "catch up" or "prepare themselves" to teach and include their children (Odom, 2002). Pre-service and in-service teacher education institutions are critical and necessary agencies with respect to encouraging, supporting and sustaining positive teacher attitudes towards and commitment to inclusive practice (Booth, Nes, & Stromstad, 2003; Purdue, Gordon-Burns, Gunn, Madden, & Surtees, 2009).

However, teacher education programmes that employ special education knowledge, discourses and practices "in order to prepare neophyte teachers for student diversity and inclusive education" are flawed (Slee, 2001, p. 168). As Slee points out, educating teachers in this way "is to formalise exclusionary special education discourses as the official knowledge of difference" (p. 168), a process that prevents the development of teachers who can be effective leaders for inclusion. The remedy, Slee continues, is for "teacher education … to explore new forms of knowledge about identity and difference and to suggest new questions that invite students to consider the pathologies of schools that enable or disable students" (p. 174).

4. Assessment

Inclusive assessment is an integral part of an inclusive curriculum. The introduction of Aotearoa New Zealand's early childhood curriculum, *Te Whāriki* (Ministry of Education, 1996), brought with it the expectation that kaiako would foreground their assessment of *all* tamariki within a sociocultural framework. *Te Whāriki* takes a holistic approach to assessment, describing it as a process that

> gives useful information about children's learning and development to the adults providing the programme and to the children and their families … [This information is] integral to making decisions on how best to meet children's needs. (Ministry of Education, 1996, p. 29)

As explored relative to the curriculum (Ministry of Education, 1996, 2005), inclusive assessment should be conducted according to the following aims and practices:

- enhance children's sense of themselves as capable people and competent learners
- reflect the holistic way that tamariki learn
- involve whānau
- reflect the many relationships that are key to children's learning and development.

Te Whāriki also establishes that if assessment determines that a child's needs are not being met, then the learning environment and planned curriculum must be modified as required.

We consider that the assessment practices associated with early intervention and special education are incompatible with the sociocultural, holistic principles that underpin *Te Whāriki*. This type of incompatibility, as Dunn (2004) argues, arises because special education typically favours developmental, normative and skills-based approaches to assessment. These approaches highlight what children cannot do rather than what they can do. They also identify intervention programmes likely to eradicate or minimise the deficits and help children progress, as much as possible, along a normal developmental continuum.

In this context, disability is constructed as a limitation on learning (Lyons, 2005; Macartney, 2008a). It is therefore essential that the early childhood and special education sectors continue to work together to find assessment models and practices that will help teachers, parents and other professionals to make good decisions about ways to support the learning of children with disabilities (see Williamson, Cullen, & Lepper, 2006, for an example of professionals co-constructing knowledge for successful inclusion).

An assessment approach evident in many of today's early childhood settings in Aotearoa New Zealand that we consider counters the deficit-based model is "learning stories", a practice that is consistent with sociocultural theories of teaching and learning and a rights-based model of disability (Carr, 2001). One of the main purposes of learning stories is to empower tamariki to engage in lifelong learning. They are also designed to involve whānau in decision making about children's learning. Because the information obtained through this approach takes account of each child's meaning-making, intentions and relationships with others in natural contexts, kaiako are better able to identify those aspects of the learning environment that may be enabling or restricting the child's learning.

5. Collaboration

The need for whānau, early childhood kaiako and other professionals (e.g., early intervention teachers, education support workers, physiotherapists, occupational therapists, speech-language therapists, case workers) to form collaborative relationships is critical if early childhood education is to be a positive experience for children with disabilities and their families. Research shows that to do otherwise places families of children with disabilities at risk of experiencing a most unhelpful and exhausting early childhood experience (MacArthur, 2004; Odom, 2002). A partnership approach provides a foundation for the sharing of knowledge, information, resources and skills (Cullen, 2009; Ministry of Education, 1996).

An important facet of collaborative teaming is that everyone is involved equally in decision-making processes. They are not recipients of an "expert discourse" of disability, whereby the "professionals" make decisions based on what is "most appropriate" or "in the best interests" of the child and family (MacArthur, 2004; Macartney, 2008a, 2008b). By working collaboratively together, all involved can problem-solve and determine inclusive techniques, activities and methods (Corbett, 2001; Foreman, 2011).

As already alluded to, some members of the teaching team may have different and conflicting viewpoints about assessment, curriculum and pedagogy relative to disability and inclusion. Such differences need to be talked through so that tamariki and their whānau are not subjected to exclusionary attitudes and practices. Ensuring continual, progressive and open collaboration among all key people may ultimately result in new knowledge and understanding, and an increased repertoire of approaches and strategies that can be used to enhance the quality of the teaching and learning environment for all children and all families. Given the importance of a partnership approach for successful inclusion, what discussions need to take place in your setting to strengthen collaborative relationships?

6. Early childhood learning environments and communities

Kaiako typically face challenges when trying to achieve the goal of progressing inclusion in their settings, and more so when they are confronted with opposition from other members of the learning community (Stark, Gordon-Burns, Purdue, Rarere-Briggs, & Turnock,

2011). Clearly, early childhood teachers have a key role in helping members of the learning community embrace and practise inclusion. The literature on inclusive education highlights certain strategies that can help teachers in this regard (Foreman, 2011; MacNaughton & Williams, 2009; Rietveld, 2010; Turnock, Gordon-Burns, Purdue, Rarere-Briggs, & Stark, 2011).This body of work advises that kaiako need to be role models for tamariki and whānau by displaying positive views and understanding of disability in their everyday practice. Acting in this way requires teachers to critically explore their own understanding, values and beliefs about disability, and the implications of these for inclusion. For example, teachers can ask themselves such questions as:

- What are tamariki learning about disability from what I say, or don't say?
- What are tamariki learning about disability from what I do, or don't do?
- What are tamariki learning about disability from the environment and from the resources I use, or don't use? (Jones & Mules, 2001).

Teachers also need to view themselves as active change agents. They need to be skilled at confronting negative stereotypes, attitudes and misconceptions about disability and inclusion and at supporting and advocating for and with families of children with disabilities. Kaiako also need to be aware of the language and terminology they use when talking about disability and tamariki with disabilities (Foreman, 2011). Part of the everyday discourse in many early childhood settings employs language that perpetuates the concept of "two kinds of education, one special and the other ... not 'special'" (Ballard, 1999, p. 167), thereby reinforcing exclusionary attitudes and behaviours. Forming an alternative language to "special needs" would seem an essential component of inclusive practice within early childhood settings (Booth et al., 2006; Glass et al., 2008).

Teachers also have the role of ensuring that the environment and play resources reflect positive and inclusionary images of disability, thus promoting disability as an ordinary aspect of life and a natural part of human diversity (Hodkinson & Vickerman, 2009). The physical environment (both indoors and outdoors) needs to meet the mobility and access requirements of tamariki and their whānau. Kaiako and management must be willing to adapt and modify their environments to make sure that this occurs.

7. Management and leadership

Because it can be a challenge to make inclusive education a reality for all, competent management and leadership are required if we are to bring about change in early childhood education that is more than tokenistic or assimilationist. Leadership for inclusion thus involves addressing some important attitudinal, theoretical, philosophical and pedagogical issues, as well as addressing issues related to resourcing and systemic change (Edmunds & Macmillan, 2010).

Managers and leaders within early childhood settings need to actively promote and model inclusive education policy in practice, support positive development and change, and effectively lead their teams in reform efforts (Mitchell, 2008). As Corbett (2001) observes,

> no teachers or support staff should feel isolated and alone in their teaching tasks but need to feel able to connect into support systems which are flexible, non-judgmental and safe spaces in which to explore challenges and barriers without blame. (p. 116)

Whānau of tamariki with disabilities likewise need to encounter management and kaiako who are not only effective leaders with respect to inclusion but are also allies and advocates (Ministry of Education, 1996). Readers who wish to explore examples of effective leadership and management for inclusion may like to refer to the work of Edmunds and Macmillan (2010) and Whalley (2008).

8. Resourcing

The right of all tamariki with disabilities to attend and receive a quality education in their local early childhood education service is likely to remain rhetoric rather than reality if not appropriately resourced. Research evidence highlights the fact that inadequate resourcing, especially funding—not only in the early childhood sector but also in the special education and health sectors—is one of the main barriers to inclusion (Macartney, 2011; Purdue, 2004). The current funding issues facing the early childhood sector will create further pressures for exclusion. It is therefore likely that lack of resourcing will continue to be used as a basis for discrimination against children with disabilities and their families in early childhood education.

In order to develop inclusion in early childhood settings for tamariki with disabilities, everyone involved in the early childhood and related sectors needs to address resourcing issues at all levels of the system, from the individual early childhood service to the political arena. The focus needs to move away from simply bringing in additional resources for children with disabilities, such as support people, to providing the means by which services can transform the structure and culture of their settings so that they enable rather than disable tamariki (Slee, 1996). The reflective questions Booth and his colleagues (2006) list in their *Index for Inclusion* may offer a starting point for discussions as teams grapple with issues related to resourcing diversity. The government, moreover, has to ensure that resourcing meets the rhetoric of legislated requirements and policies (Minister for Disability Issues, 2001).

Conclusion

In this chapter we have highlighted a range of factors that, when implemented, may help develop more inclusive environments for tamariki with disabilities and their whānau. We need to make clear, however, that these components should not be seen as a design blueprint for inclusion for these children. Rather, they need to be seen as an *"aide-memoire"* (Slee, 2004, p. 124) that can help guide dialogue about issues central to the inclusion and exclusion of *all* tamariki in education settings. We urge early childhood kaiako and management to critically and collaboratively consider the factors presented here, and to access other research and literature on inclusive education (in particular, Slee, 2011). These actions should help them to determine where they and the services they provide are situated in terms of inclusion and exclusion so that their thinking and practice can move forward.

Reforming education for inclusion is, we acknowledge, far from easy, and attempts to do so may be challenged and resisted by those who have vested interests in maintaining the status quo. We anticipate, in particular, that those who are committed to the field of special education will continue to claim that inclusion cannot (and even should not) be done (Kauffman & Hallahan, 2005). However, because part of our legislated responsibility as early childhood kaiako is to develop inclusive early childhood environments for all, it is important that we find ways to do this and thus make a difference. If inclusion for tamariki with disabilities appears not to be working in our settings, we should not think it cannot be achieved. Instead, we should be asking ourselves and our colleagues what is preventing inclusion for all and what we can do about it. We then need to act.

Finally, we note that because inclusive education is concerned with ensuring that early childhood education settings are responsive to the diversity of all tamariki and their whānau and communities, "inclusion will always be 'unfinished business'" (Ballard, cited in Corbett & Slee, 2000, p. 144). On this basis, all of us involved with early childhood education need to remain constantly mindful of and actively embrace the challenge laid down by *Te Whāriki*—that of weaving a mat for all to stand on.

References

Ballard, K. (1998). Disability and development. In A. Smith (Ed.), *Understanding children's development* (pp. 296–317). Wellington: Bridget Williams Books.

Ballard, K. (1999). Concluding thoughts. In K. Ballard (Ed.), *Inclusive education: International voices on disability and justice* (pp. 167–179). London, UK: Falmer Press.

Ballard, K. (2004). Children and disability: Special or included? *Waikato Journal of Education, 10,* 315–326.

Booth, T., Ainscow, M., & Kingston, D. (2006). *Index for inclusion: Developing play, learning and participation in early years and childcare.* Manchester, UK: Centre for Studies on Inclusive Education.

Booth, T., Nes, K., & Stromstad, M. (Eds.). (2003). *Developing inclusive teacher education.* London, UK: Routledge Falmer.

Brown, C. (1999). Parent voices on advocacy, education, disability and justice. In K. Ballard (Ed.), *Inclusive education: International voices on disability and justice* (pp. 28–42). London, UK: Falmer Press.

Carr, M. (2001). *Assessment in early childhood settings: Learning stories.* London, UK: Paul Chapman.

Corbett, J. (2001). *Supporting inclusive education: A connective pedagogy.* London, UK: RoutledgeFalmer.

Corbett, J., & Slee, R. (2000). An international conversation on inclusive education. In F. Armstrong, D. Armstrong, & L. Barton (Eds.), *Inclusive education: Policy, contexts and comparative perspectives* (pp. 133–146). London, UK: David Fulton.

Cullen, J. (2009). Adults co-constructing professional knowledge. In A. Anning, J. Cullen, & M. Fleer (Eds.), *Early childhood education: Society and culture* (2nd ed., pp. 80–90). London, UK: Sage.

Cullen, J., & Carroll-Lind, J. (2005). An inclusive approach to early intervention. In D. Fraser, R. Moltzen, & K. Ryba (Eds.), *Learners with special needs in Aotearoa New Zealand* (3rd ed., pp. 220–243). Palmerston North: Dunmore Press.

Dunn, L. (2004). Developmental assessment and learning stories in inclusive early intervention programmes: Two constructs in one context. *New Zealand Research in Early Childhood Education, 7,* 119–133.

Edmunds, A., & Macmillan, R. (2010). *Leadership for inclusion: A practical guide.* Rotterdam, The Netherlands: Sense Publishers.

Florian, L. (Ed.). (2007). *The Sage handbook of special education.* London, UK: Sage Publications.

Foreman, P. (2011). (Ed.). *Inclusion in action* (3rd ed.). Melbourne, VIC: Thomson.

Fraser, D., Moltzen, R., & Ryba, K. (Eds.). (2005). *Learners with special needs in Aotearoa New Zealand*. Palmerston North: Dunmore Press.

Fraser, D., & Shields, C. (2010). Leaders' roles in disrupting dominant discourses and promoting inclusion. In A. Edmunds & R. Macmillan (Eds.), *Leadership for inclusion: A practical guide* (pp. 7–18). Rotterdam, The Netherlands: Sense Publishers.

Glass, B., Baker, K., Ellis, R., Bernstone, H., & Hagen, B. (2008). Documenting for inclusion: How do we create an inclusive environment for all children? *Early Childhood Folio, 12*, 36–40.

Gordon-Burns, D., Purdue, K., Rarere-Briggs, B., Stark, R., & Turnock, K. (2010). Quality inclusive education for children with disabilities and their families: Learning from research. *International Journal of Equity and Innovation in Early Childhood, 18*(1), 53–68.

Gunn, A. (2003). Institutional body language: Are the messages we're sending really those we would wish for? *Early Education, 31*, 23–28.

Hodkinson, A., & Vickerman, P. (2009). *Key issues in special educational needs and inclusion*. London, UK: Sage.

Inclusive Education Action Group. (2011). *IEAG: Inclusive Education Action Group* [website]. Retrieved from http://www.ieag.org.nz

Jones, K., & Mules, R. (2001). Developing critical thinking and activism. In E. Dau (Ed.), *The anti-bias approach in early childhood* (2nd ed., pp. 191–209). Frenchs Forest, NSW: Longman.

Kauffman, J., & Hallahan, D. (2005). *Special education: What it is and why we need it*. Boston, MA: Pearson.

Lyons, L. (2005). A place for everybody?: Challenges in providing inclusive early childhood education for children with disability in Aotearoa/New Zealand. *The First Years: Ngā Tau Tuatahi: New Zealand Journal of Infant and Toddler Education, 7*(1), 16–20.

MacArthur, J. (2004). Tensions and conflicts: Experiences in parent and professional worlds. In L. Ware (Ed.), *Ideology and the politics of (in)exclusion* (pp. 166–182). New York, NY: Peter Lang.

MacArthur, J., Purdue, K., & Ballard, K. (2003). Competent and confident children? "Te Whāriki" and the inclusion of children with disabilities in early childhood education. In J. Nuttall (Ed.), *Weaving Te Whāriki: Aotearoa New Zealand's early childhood curriculum document in theory and practice* (pp. 131–160). Wellington: New Zealand Council for Educational Research.

Macartney, B. (2008a). Disabled by the discourse: Some impacts of normalising mechanisms in education and society on the lives of disabled children and their families. *New Zealand Research in Early Childhood Education, 11*, 33–50.

Macartney, B. (2008b). "If you don't know her, she can't talk": Noticing the tensions between deficit discourses and inclusive early childhood education. *Early Childhood Folio, 12*, 31–35.

Macartney, B. (2011). *Disabled by the discourse: Two families' narratives of inclusion, exclusion and resistance in education.* Unpublished doctoral thesis, University of Canterbury.

MacNaughton, G., & Williams, G. (2009). *Techniques for teaching young children: Choices for theory and practice* (3rd ed.). Frenchs Forest, NSW: Pearson Education.

Minister for Disability Issues. (2001). *New Zealand disability strategy: Making a world of difference—Whakanui oranga.* Wellington: Ministry of Health.

Ministry of Education. (1996). *Te whāriki: He whāriki mātauranga mō ngā mokopuna o Aotearoa: Early childhood curriculum.* Wellington: Learning Media.

Ministry of Education. (2005). Inclusive assessment. In Ministry of Education (Ed.), *Kei tua o te pae: Assessment for learning: Early childhood exemplars.* Wellington: Learning Media.

Mitchell, D. (2008). *What really works in special and inclusive education: Using evidence-based teaching strategies.* London, UK: Routledge.

Neilson, W. (2005). Disability: Attitudes, history and discourses. In D. Fraser, R. Moltzen, & K. Ryba (Eds.), *Learners with special needs in Aotearoa New Zealand* (3rd ed., pp. 9–21). Palmerston North: Dunmore Press.

Odom, S. (2002). *Widening the circle: Including children with disabilities in preschool programs.* New York, NY: Teachers College Press.

Purdue, K. (2004). *Inclusion and exclusion in early childhood education: Three case studies.* Unpublished doctoral thesis, University of Otago.

Purdue, K. (2006). Children and disability in early childhood education: "Special" or inclusive education? *Early Childhood Folio, 10*, 12–15.

Purdue, K., Gordon-Burns, D., Gunn, A., Madden, B., & Surtees, N. (2009). Supporting inclusion in early childhood settings: Some possibilities and problems for teacher education. *International Journal of Inclusive Education, 13*(8), 805–815.

Purdue, K., Gordon-Burns, D., Rarere-Briggs, B., Stark, R., & Turnock, K. (2011). The exclusion of children with disabilities in early childhood education in New Zealand: Issues and implications for inclusion. *Australasian Journal of Early Childhood, 36*(2), 95–103.

Rietveld, C. (2010). Early childhood inclusion: The hidden curriculum of peer relationships. *New Zealand Journal of Educational Studies*, 45(1), 17–32.

Rix, J. (2008). What's your attitude?: Inclusion and early years settings. In A. Paige Smith & A. Crafts (Eds.), *Developing reflective practice in the early years* (pp. 79–92). Maidenhead, UK: Open University Press.

Rix, J., Paige-Smith, A., & Jones, H. (2008). "Until the cows come home": Issues for early intervention activities?: Parental perspectives on the early years learning of their children with Down Syndrome. *Contemporary Issues in Early Childhood*, 9(1), 66–79.

Skrtic, T. (1995). *Disability and democracy: Reconstructing (special) education for postmodernity*. New York, NY: Teachers College Press.

Slee, R. (1996). Clauses of conditionality: The "reasonable" accommodation of language. In L. Barton (Ed.), *Disability and society: Emerging issues and insights* (pp. 10–122). London, UK: Prentice Hall.

Slee, R. (2001). Social justice and the changing directions in educational research: The case of inclusive education. *International Journal of Inclusive Education*, 5(2/3), 167–177.

Slee, R. (2004). Closing the gap. *International Journal of Inclusive Education*, 8(2), 123–124.

Slee, R. (2011). *The irregular school: Exclusion, schooling and inclusive education*. London, UK: Routledge.

Stark, R., Gordon-Burns, D., Purdue, K., Rarere-Briggs, B., & Turnock, K. (2011). Other parents' perceptions of disability and inclusion in early childhood education: Implications for the teacher's role in creating inclusive communities. *He Kupu*, 2(1), 4–18.

Turnock, K., Gordon-Burns, D., Purdue, K., Rarere-Briggs, B., & Stark, R. (2011). "I'm scared of that baby": How adults and environments contribute to children's positive or negative understandings and experiences of disability in early childhood settings. *New Zealand Research in Early Childhood Education Journal*, 14, 23–37.

Whalley, M. (2008). *Leading practice in early years settings*. Exeter, UK: Learning Matters.

Williamson, D., Cullen, J., & Lepper, C. (2006). Checklists to narratives in special education. *Australian Journal of Early Childhood*, 31(2), 20–29.

CHAPTER 10

Puzzling over inclusion: Concluding remarks

Diane Gordon-Burns, Alexandra C. Gunn, Kerry Purdue and Nicola Surtees

This volume has engaged with the problems and promise associated with practising inclusive education within the context of early childhood education in Aotearoa New Zealand. Writing from within frameworks informed by sociocultural and poststructural theory, the contributing authors have explored issues of difference, diversity, inclusion and exclusion from multiple perspectives—Māori and cultural responsiveness, sexualities, Te Tiriti o Waitangi and biculturalism, economic disadvantage, age, interculturalism, gender, religion and disability. The authors illuminate how people's everyday language and practices build barriers to inclusive education. The authors also raise awareness of how all of us involved in early childhood education can embrace difference and diversity in ways that make our practice more socially just.

In this chapter we reflect on what can be learned from the perspectives of the contributors to this book. We consider, in particular, views about how and why exclusion occurs, the values and attitudes that facilitate inclusionary practice, and the issues and challenges that still confront inclusive education in this country. Selectively sampling from the chapters, we synthesise key messages for inclusion and in so doing begin to engage more fully with the kinds of cultural politics for change that we and others (e.g., Allan, 2008; Ballard, 1999; Slee, 2011) deem necessary if we are to progress inclusive education now and in the future.

What have we learned?

Inclusion and exclusion: How and why they occur

As discussed in the introductory chapter, power can be thought of as instrumental to the conditions for inclusion and exclusion. Power is observed through surveillance, normalising judgements and examination. The standards by which we judge and examine— and by which we are judged and examined—reflect dominant values, attitudes and beliefs. The workings of power thus mediate experiences of domination and oppression.

Across the chapters we have learned that discrimination is typically justified on the basis that some people are "different" in some way from the groups or individuals claiming a dominant place in society. People viewed in this way risk being rejected and excluded because their differences are viewed negatively and are therefore neither valued nor wanted. When kaiako, tamariki and whānau are labelled and categorised in ways that negate their "normality" and/ or are viewed as "other", people not so labelled may undermine, whether covertly or overtly, their access to and participation in an equitable and socially just early childhood education in their local community.

This explanation for the presence of inclusionary or exclusionary practices in early childhood education rests on the notion that values, attitudes, language and practices act as enablers for or barriers to learning and participation. It reminds us, too, that these values, attitudes, languages and practices can change, which means that power can be seen as a dynamic, not a static, force. It circulates among individuals and groups in, as Foucault described, a capillary-like fashion (Faubion, 2002) that touches us all. We can, accordingly, see inclusion as a communal responsibility, reliant on relationships for its success. Interactions in early childhood settings between more experienced and less experienced community members are instructive for the ways in which they communicate particular values, attitudes and beliefs. In order to build communities where everyone feels they belong, all involved need to successfully negotiate different world views and perspectives.

Herein lies the potential for pursuing inclusion. Each time new whānau, tamariki or kaiako join the community, they bring something different to the mix. By learning with and from one another, community members who are open to diversity and difference will likely welcome this opportunity to build the community a little differently each time someone new enters it. They fully recognise each community member's uniqueness and thus value his or her contributions. For us and our colleagues in this book, the ability to accommodate continual shifts in power relations in response to encountering differing views and ways of being is largely what inclusive education is all about.

The engagement throughout this book with a social-constructionist view of knowledge production makes clear for us that what gets taken as normal or true in any given situation is the result of countless human choices and interpretations. The chapter authors show how particular constructions of "normal" culture, ability, sexuality, religion, gender and wealth arise and influence contemporary early childhood practices. They also show how inequitable relations between Māori, Pasifika and migrant populations and Pākehā New Zealanders can lead to disengagement, failure and exclusion within and from Aotearoa New Zealand early childhood settings and schools. Revealing how dominant constructions support practices that work in the interests of some ideas, knowledge and understandings while simultaneously problematising others allows us to appreciate that certain individuals and groups can perceive their social realities very differently from the realities that others consider are normal or proper or true.

Richard Manning's discussion in Chapter 4 of the teaching of the haka "Ka Mate" in his son's early childhood centre illustrates this point. The teachers in Richard's account possessed a strong sense of ownership of this haka as a cultural "icon, made famous by the All Blacks" (p. 63). Richard and others in the centre were, however, highly uncomfortable about its teaching—Richard because of his sensitivity to the (at that time unresolved) Ngāti Toa claim to this haka, and his son's friend's whānau because of their location relative to historical intertribal warfare. Assuming that the teachers' discourse about *Ka Mate*—it is a famous cultural (as in sporting) icon—had become dominant in the early childhood centre community, as appeared to be the case in Richard's experience, it would have left other discourses and points of view about *Ka Mate* marginalised. Without an opportunity to be heard, or to have their different points of view meaningfully discussed, Richard and others were denied an opportunity to share their knowledge fully and to contribute to the learning of all in the centre. They were left frustrated and (although this was probably not realised by the teachers concerned) subjected to a form of exclusion.

Richard's story helps us to appreciate that an individual's different positioning in relation to a field of dominant norms, assumptions, values and truths can leave him or her discouraged, troubled, rendered abnormal and marked as other—or not. But we also need to recognise that shifts across or between positions can be rapidly effected relative to the discourses being deployed at any given time. An example of this is evident in Nicola Surtees' chapter (Chapter 3) when she introduces us to Genevieve, Lynley, Pascal and Shamus.

Nicola shows how Genevieve and Lynley's desire to parent in a nuclear family structure (which re-inscribes heteronormativity) places limits on Pascal and Shamus. The women, by privileging heteronormativity through their expressed desire to raise their children as if they were a traditional nuclear family, construct themselves as parents. This situation leaves little room for the men to be recognised as parents both within and outside the family structure. We see, therefore, that relationships between adults, and relationships between adults and tamariki, are changeable and multiply manifest, depending on the discourses in play. Remaining cognisant of how various discourses include and exclude is thus an important component of progressing inclusion.

The authors who contributed to this book have also demonstrated the ways in which dominant constructions in their domains of interest (e.g., gender, disability, interculturalism) become institutionalised and taken for granted. Alex Gunn's genealogy (Chapter 7) of a discourse of disadvantage as it relates to boys and men in Aotearoa New Zealand early childhood education shows how. As Alex explains, gender issues in education shifted from a 1970s and 1980s emphasis on achievement and equity for girls, to the "boy turn" of the 1990s, and on to growing alarm in the 2000s over boys' (lack of) success and the plight of men who teach. This framing of gender issues across time makes evident how media, political debate, public policy and research emanating from different social spheres deploy different gender discourses that led to the construction of new "truths". Alex also discusses how members of particular social groups actively maintain particular points of view and norms about genders, and how resistance to these is made possible by active engagement with counter discourses, such as those accepting of gender diversity.

In summarising the lessons learned about how and why inclusion and exclusion occur, we reiterate that power relations drive the conditions for both. Manifesting in myriad ways, power mediates experiences of oppression. Those who are oppressed face discrimination because their "difference" (a different world view, different ability, different sexuality and so forth) is viewed negatively—it is undervalued, refused or positioned as a problem to be overcome. This is an effect of discourses that construct difference as deficit. In such a context, those without perceptible differences are assumed to be "one of us" (in the dominant position) and therefore not subject to the kinds of scrutiny, examination or normalising judgements experienced by the "other". These relationships between power, knowledge and discourse are therefore important for understanding how inclusion and exclusion come to occur.

Early childhood settings that construct difference positively are more likely to practise inclusion for all. These dynamic communities in which members' values, attitudes and language act as enablers for learning and participation welcome differences and the opportunities these afford members to learn together while successfully negotiating diverse world views and perspectives. By working within a social-constructionist world view, recognising community and reflectively engaging with discourses, we are open to the fact that, over time, values, attitudes, language and practices can evolve and change; opportunities to practise in ever more inclusive and socially just ways are therefore always upon us.

Values and attitudes underpinning inclusive and exclusionary practice

All our chapter authors engage with Te Whāriki (Ministry of Education, 1996) for its "touchstone" value regarding inclusion, its attention to differing values, attitudes and norms, and its response to contemporary sociocultural perspectives on learning. Given this engagement, it is not surprising that the contributing authors view teacher values and attitudes as instrumental to inclusive or exclusionary practices in early childhood education. The curriculum instructs kaiako to protect and enhance children's mana and to provide, in concert with whānau, early childhood settings that support children to participate fully in the communities and societies of which they are a part. To do this, kaiako must value learning (their own and the learning of others), recognise that the knowledge required for progressing inclusion may lie beyond their immediate expertise, and welcome democracy, flexibility and uncertainty.

Di Gordon-Burns, Kerry Purdue, Benita Rarere-Briggs, Robyn Stark and Karen Turnock make this point in their chapter (Chapter 9) when arguing that learning from one another plays a large role in progressing inclusive education for children with disabilities. As these authors note, critical dialogue among community members about suggested strategies and practices, along with thoughtful engagement with a range of relevant research, can help move thinking and practice forward, but only if everyone is heard. Mindful that different community members are likely to harbour alternative points of view about how best to meet the challenges of inclusive education in any given situation, Di, Kerry, Benita, Robyn and Karen argue for problem solving and collaborative action that lead to the building of relationships and trust.

Focusing more explicitly on the notion of difference, Gina Colvin, Darcey Dachyshyn and Jo Togiaso (Chapter 6) argue that teachers should welcome differences as gifts. For Gina, Darcey and Jo, these gifts can be construed as—to use González, Moll and Amanti's (2005) concept—"funds of knowledge". This concept recognises that knowledge which is most valued by a community is that which comes from and belongs to all members of it, rather than to the dominant majority only. In the authors' words, kaiako in early childhood settings would do well to "live mindfully, presently and openly in each and every moment and encounter that comes [their] way" (p. 108), and in doing so would likely find themselves in a "field of potentially positive tension" (p. 109), protective of different ways of knowing and resistant to homogenising approaches and exclusionary practices.

The argument at this point is not against teacher expertise and knowledge *per se*, but rather for kaiako to perceive value in welcoming knowledge and expertise emanating from different orientations. Kaiako who work from this position are open to diversity and therefore more likely to have the ability to work thoughtfully with and draw from the variety of expertise and world views available within and beyond themselves. Moss (2010, p. 15) gives this explanation:

> The educator cannot look to a profession to provide an objectively true body of knowledge. Rather, to be professional means being able to construct knowledge from diverse sources, involving awareness of paradigmatic plurality, curiosity and border crossing, and acknowledging that knowledge is always partial, perspectival and provisional.

Such thinking gives merit to the claim that preserving and protecting the agency and ability of all learners—both experienced and novice—in the early childhood community is a valuable means of progressing inclusion. Glynne Mackey and Colleen Lockie make this point in Chapter 5 as they discuss the importance for inclusive education of seeing children as "human *beings*, not human *becomings*" (p. 90) in the early childhood context. According to Glynne and Colleen, protecting democracy through pedagogies that support tamariki and their whānau to fully participate in daily decision making about the things that affect them is an important factor in ameliorating the effects of impoverishment. Kaiako who value individuals' rights to participation and the strength that can be built from working collectively are thus likely to be working in the interests of inclusive education.

In summarising the learning about values and attitudes underlying inclusive and exclusionary practices, the chapter authors show that kaiako who value difference as positive and who carry an attitude protective of one's rights to full participation are progressing inclusion. When the culture of an early childhood setting is one that supports teachers and its other members to draw on all the expertise and world views available to it and then to use that expertise to benefit the broader community, that setting has the wherewithal to find solutions to problems for all. The authors recognise that such work is difficult and complex, but they maintain that this is vital for building relationships of trust and openness. In the next section we endeavour to respond to some of the complexities in this process.

Issues and challenges associated with inclusive education

One message that comes through strongly in this book is that working towards inclusionary practices is a demanding but rewarding endeavour—for ourselves, for those we work with and teach, and for the wider society. The crux of this process is our ability and capacity to engage in close, recurrent examination of our own values, attitudes and beliefs and to explore our own complicity with respect to exclusionary practices. At issue, too, is the ways in which others, including colleagues, management, tamariki, whānau and the wider community, sometimes work against efforts to advance inclusive practices.

Calling ourselves to account requires effort. It is exacting and, to use that commonplace expression, is easier said than done. This process can have a particularly sobering effect on us when it makes us aware of the many and varied ways we actively exclude—despite trying not to. Sometimes we desire the very things that exclude. As Alex and Nicola have previously suggested (Gunn & Surtees, 2004), all of us may desire—and thus reinforce and reproduce—the oppressive because it is familiar and authenticates particular ways of being; if our way is "right", we don't have to accommodate the ways of others. But if we don't actively critique and reflect on our own attitudes and behaviours, holding them up for scrutiny against other possible ways of being and doing, we have no means of generating the commitment, motivation and momentum to work towards something different. Until we recognise how we are implicated in oppression, we have neither the insight with which to understand "difference" nor the strength to change our thinking and practices.

Sonja Macfarlane and Angus Macfarlane's chapter (Chapter 2) stresses the importance of such critique with reference to educational outcomes for Māori tamariki. Sonja and Angus point out that kaiako must "reflect on and interrogate the what, why, how and who of their teaching theory and praxis—to consider *what* is included in the curriculum, *why* it is important, *how* it is constructed and operationalised, and *who* it will benefit" (p. 23). Opportunity for kaiako to listen to whānau and realise with them their aspirations for their tamariki is unlikely in settings where Māori world views and values are marginalised. If teachers create and operationalise curriculum by drawing exclusively on Western theories and knowledge, they risk homogenising practice. In these kinds of contexts, being able to recognise the uniqueness of each child's mana and his or her place in the world will remain, as Sonja and Angus explain, a challenge.

But even when we have critiqued, reflected, changed as best we can, others may oppose, counteract or undermine our attempts to advance inclusive practices. Colleagues, management, tamariki, whānau, the community may offer little or no support; they may be hostile to or resist our work. If we challenge them, we risk conflict—a daunting prospect for many. Intervening when resistance comes from families and the wider community presents a particular conundrum. How can we respect the rights of families and communities to have and uphold their own values and beliefs about difference and diversity when these conflict with our agenda to embrace difference and diversity as enriching for us all?

Bradley Hannigan's work (Chapter 8) raises an interesting discussion on this point. In his consideration of decisions by families to actively hide a core aspect of their identity—their religious affiliation—Bradley highlights the dilemma of how kaiako might respect the choices that families sometimes make to minimise aspects of their own difference so that they "fit in". Teachers' attempts towards inclusion may well compromise families' sense of security and wellbeing. The question of whose interests take priority and when makes for a terrain that is difficult to negotiate. Once again, we counsel the need for critical conversations, not only because they tend to illuminate the knowledge and practices systematically obscured by people's language and actions, but also because they keep us mindful of our own values about and tolerance for world views, knowledge and understandings that differ from our own. And once aware of the silencing of aspects of identity, we would also do well to ask ourselves, how much of a compromise is too much for the people concerned?

Another challenge implicitly conveyed in this book is that of accommodating the realisation that the work of inclusion can never be complete. If we accept that early childhood settings continually change as new members join and different understandings, values and beliefs are voiced, then inclusion cannot be a static ideological construct, or totalising in effect. It cannot be addressed through a one-size-fits-all set of strategies that kaiako implement when they meet diverse people, lifestyles and viewpoints previously unmet in the early childhood setting, or when they are confronted by incidents of discrimination and exclusion. Inclusion is invariably messy, uncertain and complex.

Inclusive practice is therefore imbued with a sense of *doing* rather than of having been *done*: it can (and therefore should) be approached from multiple pathways every single day. Such work requires a "certain attitude of mind" (Moss, 2010, p. 16). Positioned and understood in this way—as a complex, continual process that demands ongoing action and involves many possible ways of moving forward—inclusion becomes a very ambitious and optimistic project. Allan (2008, p. 164) is unequivocal on this point:

> For inclusion to be a possibility, we must be ready to say yes to it and promise to say yes to it again … The affirmation of inclusion without a repetition amounts to a 'wait and see', a 'maybe', which can quickly retreat to the refusals that we have seen. So, if we do want inclusion to happen, we need to say yes with the confidence that it will be 'repeated in the quiet, steady beat of tomorrow and tomorrow' (Caputo, 1997, p. 188). So we can never be done with the project of inclusion and must continue to puzzle over it together with those who stand to gain most.

In summarising the lessons learned about the issues and challenges associated with inclusive education, we are struck afresh by our (the editors') mutual belief that inclusion, as a daily yet always incomplete practice, brings continual challenges, not all of which can be predicted from the outset. This work is demanding, but it is also rewarding, as opportunities to grow personally and professionally abound. Regular examination of values, attitudes and practices must be to the fore if we are to compensate for complicity with exclusionary practices and to offset the ways in which others can undermine efforts to change previously unquestioned practices. *Doing* inclusion, as Allan (2008) reminds us, is indeed repetitive, puzzling work.

Engaging with cultural politics for change

Perhaps the main, yet relatively simple, message to come from the work set down in this book is that working for inclusion with and for very young tamariki and their whānau means being receptive to what they bring to the early childhood learning community. We use the term "receptive" when perhaps we would prefer "welcoming" because inclusion does not mean having to accommodate attitudes and behaviours that work against social justice and equity. As stated earlier, practising inclusion involves continually negotiating different world views, perspectives and values; as such, this work is cultural and political. It entails the constant care of a climate in which important meanings and values about difference, diversity, inclusion and exclusion are created and contested. Negativity about difference and diversity will arise and needs to be addressed by the members of early childhood communities in ways that acknowledge difficulties but that preserve inclusion and people's rights. Robinson (2005, p.182) neatly encapsulates this point when she uses the term "community courage" to describe such whole-setting or community approaches to social justice work in education. We would add to this that the work is a "community responsibility". Teachers who act in and with community are essential if the complexities and uncertainties inherent in such disruptive work are not to immobilise those who view it as too hard or who invite one-off "quick-fix", "tick-box" type solutions. As Robinson and Jones Diaz (2006, p. 174) state, such solutions "may appeal to many as a way of masking or obscuring difficult issues, but ultimately they will not provide a sufficient means for effectively dealing with issues of diversity and difference."

While the particular perspectives evident in each chapter of this book can and should be used to progress thinking and practice with respect to inclusion—and exclusion—in early childhood education settings (and beyond), we caution against taking any of them as a definitive account of the ways difference and diversity are experienced and potentially responded to in early childhood education. Almost daily we, as early childhood kaiko and teacher educators, continue to learn about and are surprised by the implications of the multiple manifestations of difference and diversity. As our communities change, so too do those aspects of difference and diversity within them. This understanding brings relevance to how we conceptualise and practise for inclusion. If our conceptualisations of inclusion become "fixed" to those aspects present in any one community at a particular point in time or, in the case of this book, to those perspectives the authors have explored, we risk assuming that inclusion has been "done".

This is a pitfall that we have discussed elsewhere (Purdue, Gordon-Burns, Gunn, Madden, & Surtees, 2009), but we make the point again here because it is an important one. Despite our own efforts to challenge a narrow conception of inclusion—one that student-teachers frequently define as those aspects of difference and diversity covered in course content—we still struggle with such constructions each year. While our work in initial teacher education may have helped shift the boundaries of inclusion beyond the single focus on disability typical of many teacher-education programmes in this country (Morton & Gordon, 2006), our experiences draw attention to the danger of fixing inclusion to particular perspectives, both those named in this book and others unnamed here. The danger is privileging some voices and perspectives while re-inscribing the exclusion of others, arguably of those tamariki and whānau not mentioned in this volume.

We naturally hope that those of you who have read this book will consider the particular "differences" addressed in its chapters in relation to your own thinking and practice. However, we also urge you to use what has been written here to prompt critical discussions on matters of injustice and exclusion in early childhood education more broadly and then, as an outcome of that work, to apply new understandings in ways that progress inclusion. Such activity will extend the scope of this book *beyond* consideration of the perspectives named herein and lessen the privileging of some voices over others. Consider, as examples, these questions:

- What have you learned from—or do you even agree with— poststructural and sociocultural understandings that position difference and diversity as socially and culturally constructed?

- How might analysing discourses help you to understand difference and diversity relative to perspectives not considered in this book (e.g., gifted and talented children and their families, children and/or family members who are obese)?
- Which attitudes towards difference and diversity documented in this book resonate for your own practice and the practice of those with whom you work?
- Which strategies discussed in the book do you consider useful for creating inclusive curriculum in the early childhood learning communities you engage in? How might you employ them?
- How receptive is the climate of your early childhood setting towards differing world views, values, attitudes and beliefs? How do you know?
- What policies and practices facilitate or limit inclusive attitudes, not only in your workplace but also in your own whānau and community? What, if anything, needs to change? How could you facilitate that change?
- What might you need to be mindful of when challenging discrimination as it arises in the early childhood learning communities of which you are a part?
- How best might you help the critical conversations to begin?

By prompting reflection on questions such as these and then calling for appropriate action in response to the answers, this book moves beyond any pretence of being a definitive work on the "how to" of inclusion in Aotearoa New Zealand early childhood education (and it was never our intention that it should be). Instead, we position the book as a *tool* that kaiako and others participating in early childhood education can put to use as they build their own ability to think about and practise inclusion. In this way, the book can never be complete. Addressing all possible perspectives and covering all aspects of difference and diversity are surely impossible tasks and inconsistent with the conceptualisation of inclusion offered here;

namely, an ongoing process, a journey. In our view, assuming an endpoint to that journey would risk undermining it.

Conclusion

In this book, we and our colleagues looked at who is included, who is excluded and why, from within the contexts of early childhood education. We addressed some of the issues and challenges surrounding inclusion and remained mindful of the old adage that doing nothing (when discrimination, injustice and exclusion occur) is doing something. Our referencing throughout this book to sociocultural thinking and poststructural practices provided us all with a useful framework from which to critically examine the notions of inclusion, equity and social justice. More specifically, this approach allowed us to consider how these notions are understood, might be understood and even should be understood with respect to the present philosophical, policy and regulatory orientations of early childhood education in Aotearoa New Zealand.

Slee's (2011) comment that inclusion must be advanced on many levels if we are to achieve fair and socially just education with and for tamariki and whānau makes us even more aware of the major role that those of us involved in early childhood education can play in shaping possibilities for the future. Ours is the domain in which many families first encounter formal education settings. If we can strive for full participation here, we may well come to expect it in other contexts. We hope this book inspires readers to work towards this end.

> He ahiahi pokopoko, he ata hī tore.
>
> As the fire is extinguished, the light of dawn shines through—there is always hope.

References

Allan, J. (2008). *Rethinking inclusive education: The philosophers of difference in practice*. London, UK: Springer.

Ballard, K. (Ed.). (1999). *Inclusive education: International voices on disability and justice*. London, UK: Falmer Press.

Faubion, D. (Ed.). (2002). *Michel Foucault—Power: Essential works of Foucault 1954–1984* (Vol. 3, R. Hurley and others, trans). London, UK: Penguin Books.

González, N., Moll, C. M., & Amanti, C. (2005). *Funds of knowledge: Theorizing practices in households, communities, and classrooms*. Mahwah, NJ: Lawrence Erlbaum Associates.

Gunn, A. C., & Surtees, N. (2004). Engaging with dominance and knowing our desires: New possibilities for addressing sexualities matters in early childhood education. *New Zealand Journal of Educational Leadership, 19*, 79–91.

Ministry of Education. (1996). *Te whāriki: He whāriki mātauranga mō ngā mokopuna o Aotearoa: Early childhood curriculum*. Wellington: Learning Media.

Morton, M., & Gordon, L. (2006). *Inclusive education in Aotearoa: What are we doing in initial teacher education, professional learning and development?: Final report to NZCCS*. Christchurch: Christchurch College of Education.

Moss, P. (2010). We cannot continue as we are: The educator in an education for survival. *Contemporary Issues in Early Childhood, 11*(1), 8–19.

Purdue, K., Gordon-Burns, D., Gunn, A., Madden, B., & Surtees, N. (2009). Supporting inclusion in early childhood settings: Some possibilities and problems for teacher education. *International Journal of Inclusive Education, 13*(8), 805–815.

Robinson, K. (2005). Doing anti-homophobia and anti-heterosexism in early childhood education: Moving beyond the immobilising impacts of "risks", "fears" and "silences": Can we afford not to? *Contemporary Issues in Early Childhood, 6*(2), 175–188.

Robinson, K., & Jones Diaz, C. (2006). *Diversity and difference in early childhood education: Issues for theory and practice*. Maidenhead, UK: Open University Press.

Slee, R. (2011). *The irregular school: Exclusion, schooling and inclusive education*. London, UK: Routledge.

Notes on contributors

GINA COLVIN, Ngāti Porou, Ngā Puhi, is a lecturer at the University of Canterbury, Christchurch. Her research and teaching interests include cultural studies, colonial discourse, critical pedagogy and whiteness theory.
Email: gina.colvin@canterbury.ac.nz

DARCEY M. DACHYSHYN has taught early childhood education in Canada, the United States and Aotearoa New Zealand (at the University of Canterbury). Darcey's research interests are in the areas of newcomer resettlement, interculturalism and cultural studies.
Email: darcey.dachyshyn@gmail.com

DIANE GORDON-BURNS, Ngāti Māhuta, Tainui, lectures, teaches and conducts research into early childhood education at the University of Canterbury, Christchurch. Her research encompasses bicultural curriculum, inclusive education, and a Tainui perspective on oral traditions about significant women.
Email: diane.gordon-burns@canterbury.ac.nz

ALEXANDRA GUNN recently moved from a position at the University of Canterbury and now writes and teaches about early childhood education at the University of Otago. She also conducts research in this area. Formerly a teacher of child care, Alex's research interests embrace inclusive education, educational assessment, social justice, and early childhood pedagogy (including teachers' beliefs and practices).
Email: alex.gunn@otago.ac.nz

BRADLEY HANNIGAN, a former lecturer in early childhood education at the University of Canterbury, is currently a senior education advisor at the Nelson Tasman Kindergarten Association, where he is responsible for overseeing multiple action-research projects and working with teachers to improve outcomes for children. His research interests include pedagogical pragmatism, adult education, philosophy of education and organisation leadership.
Email: drbradley.hannigan@nnkindy.org.nz

COLLEEN LOCKIE is an employee of Kidsfirst Kindergartens in Christchurch. She previously lectured in early childhood programmes at Christchurch College of Education and the University of Canterbury. Her interests include practitioner research, professional development, education for sustainability, peace in education, and early childhood assessment and curriculum.
Email: colleen.lockie@kidsfirst.org.nz

SONJA MACFARLANE, Ngāi Tahu, Ngāti Waewae, is a researcher at the Health Sciences Centre, University of Canterbury. Her research pursuits focus on enhancing social, cultural and educational outcomes for Māori learners. Sonja is currently completing her doctoral thesis in the area of culturally responsive pedagogy and evidence-based practice.
Email: sonja.macfarlane@canterbury.ac.nz

ANGUS MACFARLANE, Te Arawa, is Professor of Māori Research at the University of Canterbury. His research activities focus on exploring cultural concepts and strategies that influence educational practice. In 2010 he was conferred the national NZARE Tohu Pae Tawhiti award for his outstanding contribution to Māori research.
Email: angus.macfarlane@canterbury.ac.nz

GLYNNE MACKEY is an early childhood lecturer at the University of Canterbury, where she teaches and conducts research in the area of education for sustainability and social justice. Her main research interests encompass national and international collaborations on sustainability in the early years and reorienting teacher education towards sustainability.
Email: glynne.mackey@canterbury.ac.nz

RICHARD MANNING co-ordinates the Treaty of Waitangi Education Programme at the University of Canterbury College of Education. He previously worked as a claims inquiry facilitator/researcher at the Waitangi Tribunal. Richard has also completed research for the Department of Māori Affairs, Iwi Transition Agency and the State Services Commission.
Email: richard.manning@canterbury.ac.nz

KERRY PURDUE is a lecturer in early childhood education at the University of Canterbury and a former teacher. She is interested in inclusive early childhood education and social justice issues. A researcher and writer in the area of disability, inclusion and exclusion in early childhood education, Kerry is of Ngāi Tahu and Ngāti Māmoe descent.
Email: kerry.purdue@canterbury.ac.nz

BENITA RARERE-BRIGGS, Ngāti Kahungunu, Ngāti Porou, is a lecturer at the University of Canterbury, where she works with preservice early childhood students. Benita's interests lie in how whānau voices are heard in early childhood settings, and in the transitions that children experience when going into, within and leaving early childhood settings.
Email: benita.rarere-briggs@canterbury.ac.nz

ROBYN STARK teaches in the early childhood teacher education programme at the University of Canterbury. She has worked in a range of early childhood settings. Her research interests are in the areas of disability studies and the role and place of the Treaty of Waitangi in teacher education.
Email: robyn.stark@canterbury.ac.nz

NICOLA SURTEES lectures in early childhood education at the University of Canterbury, teaching in the Bachelor of Teaching and Learning degree. Formerly an early childhood teacher, Nicola researches and writes in the areas of social justice, inclusion and heteronormativity in early childhood education and, more recently, in the area of family studies.
Email: nicola.surtees@canterbury.ac.nz

JO TOGIASO, mother to three girls, has taught in early childhood centres, including a licensed Tongan centre and a Samoan A'oga Amata centre, in Christchurch for over 12 years. She currently works at the University of Canterbury and is passionate about indigenous learning, and about Pasifika early childhood education in particular.
Email: joeana.togiaso@canterbury.ac.nz

KAREN TURNOCK works with preservice early childhood teacher education students at the University of Canterbury. Her research interests lie in the areas of inclusion, assessment, infants and toddlers, and teacher change.
Email: karen.turnock@canterbury.ac.nz

Index